A MOTHER
NEVER FORGETS

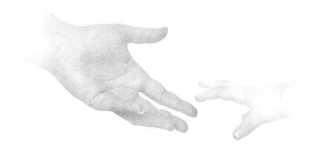

NANCY HANNAN

Editorial development and creative design support by Ascent:
www.itsyourlifebethere.com

I dedicate this book to
all "other" mothers.

In his book, "Love and Will,"
Rollo May, a leading Psychotherapist, quotes
an ancient Abyssinian Noblewoman:

The day when a woman enjoys her first love cuts her in two. The man is the same after his first love as he was before. The woman is from the day of her first love, another. That continues so all through life. The man spends a night by a woman and goes away. His life and body are always the same. The woman conceives. As a mother she is another person than a woman without a child.

She carries the fruit of the night nine months long in her body. Something grows. Something grows into her life that never again departs from it. She is a mother. She is and remains a mother even though her child dies.

For at one time she carried the child under her heart. And it does not go out of her heart ever again. Not even when it is gone. All this a man does not know... he does not know the difference before love and after love, before motherhood and after motherhood. Only a woman can know that and speak of that.

PROLOGUE

SOMETIMES THE GREAT journeys of life begin when you least expect them.

I hoisted my nearly eight month pregnant body onto the bus for my weekly OB visit that day in June, 1956. I was only twenty-five, but the shortness of breath made me feel like I was ninety. It was an exceptionally hot summer, and that, combined with the excess fluid I'd retained made any exertion uncomfortable.

I was looking forward to this visit in the hope my physician would be able to relieve my symptoms. As a nurse, I blamed the fatigue and shortness of breath on depletion of potassium due to the diuretics I was given to help lower my blood pressure. Hopefully, the doctor would have a different solution for my problem.

As I lay back on the examining table I felt nervous. During the previous visit, he had suggested I get off my feet, but I needed money to pay the rent so continued to work in the OR. I thought if I took the bus instead of walking to work that would help. I certainly hoped the baby was doing well and that the strain I was under was not affecting the child negatively in any way.

After listening to the baby's heart, my obstetrician told me to meet him in his office.

Suddenly I felt uncomfortable and not just physically. I was nervous about what he might say about my situation—not only my pregnancy but my life situation.

Being an unwed, pregnant woman in the fifties was totally unacceptable. Young women caught in this mistake were usually hidden or sent away. Students 'went abroad' for a semester, others went to live in homes for unwed mothers, or went to live with 'a very ill relative in another state so they could help.' The lucky ones married the baby's father.

This was a period that advocated conformity and conventionality. Young women, some only in their teens, were branded as Scarlet. The birth certificate of an infant born to an unwed mother was stamped across it in red letters, "Illegitimate." Eighty percent of unwed mothers gave up their babies. Anyone who had knowledge of the unfortunate situation was compelled to keep the secret. The child was never to know it was adopted, and the mothers were told they would "forget." Forced to give up their babies, these women returned to society deeply scarred.

These were the times and circumstances in which I found myself pregnant and unwed. Determined *not* to conform to the times, I thought I could form my own plan and determine my own destiny.

With this determination, I had left a comfortable nursing position in a small hospital outside Philadelphia, and gone to work at a much larger hospital in the inner city where I did not know anyone. I added "Mrs." in front of my name, purchased a gold band, and told everyone, "My husband is overseas." No one at the hospital ever knew any different. I was determined to maintain as normal a life as possible in my unacceptable condition.

What I did not count on were other, greater forces, which would determine my life's path for me and the life path of my unborn child.

Now, as I sat across the desk from my obstetrician he delivered some difficult news.

"Nancy," he said, "your toxemia is getting worse. Your blood pressure is over 200, you have excess protein in your urine, and your liver enzymes are elevated. The only known treatment for toxemia at this time is to deliver the baby... and it's too early. You really must get off your feet. And...," he added after a moment's silence, "You need to tell someone in the family that you are pregnant." I don't want to have to tell a mother that her daughter died in childbirth when she did not even know her daughter was pregnant. You have less than a fifty percent chance of surviving, and you need to make arrangements for the baby. If you believe your family will not care for the baby, then you must seriously consider adoption." He was blunt and to the point. "Sorry to have to say this to you, but you could die. "

All I could think of at that moment was that if I had to give up this baby, I had already given up the father, whom I loved, I wanted to die. I had nothing to live for. But most definitely did not want my baby to die.

On the other hand I was already in a predicament. The father was a respected physician, with a reputation and a livelihood at stake. No one who knew me knew I was pregnant. My family was 150 miles away in Washington DC. They were intensely catholic and would probably disown me. Even if I were to survive the delivery, adoption was not an option, as far as I was concerned.

I sat there in numb silence. The doctor—perhaps sensing my hesitancy and uncertainty, said, "Think about it. I'll help you in any way I can."

"I have a patient who desperately wants to adopt and has been waiting for a 'good' baby. I rely on a lawyer who will facilitate all legal ends of the adoption… It will be very easy and the adopting parents will assume the cost."

I had barely one month to deal with this emotional nightmare and let him know my decision.

Even as his words unsettled me, I also sat there thinking, *He can't be serious*. Was I really in danger of dying? Early in the pregnancy he suggested that adoption would be the best decision for me and the baby… now he had a patient who wanted a "good" baby. I began to doubt his motives. As chief of obstetrics at a large hospital in the City, and though this man was well educated and respected, he couldn't be deceiving me—could he?

Emotionally and physically exhausted, I was forced to stand the entire way home on a full bus. Trying to balance myself in the aisle, I tried, unsuccessfully, not to cry. No one seemed to even notice that I was very pregnant...and upset. I felt invisible.

Once off the bus I headed for my apartment near the Art Museum. My thoughts were racing. To me, giving up my child to adoption would be worse than death because, unlike actually losing a child to sickness or tragedy, there would be no closure.

As I walked home, I passed the Convent of the Pink Nuns, a group of cloistered nuns who wear a pink habit, and a thought crossed my mind: *Maybe they will care for my baby until I get well.* And what if I did not make it? Were nuns capable of raising an infant or would the child end up in an orphanage anyway, or be shuttled from foster home to foster home? Outside the high fence that protected them from the real world, and with my hand on the doorbell for the longest time...I just stood there. I was miserable.

At least ring the bell, it won't hurt to ask, I kept telling myself. And then another part of my mind said, *This is a stupid request.*

My hand came away from the doorbell, and I continued my miserable walk home. With each step I sank closer to despair.

The Cathedral of Saints Peter and Paul was a block from my place, so I stopped and went inside. Kneeling in prayer, I asked God to show me what to do.

Inside me, there was only turmoil... and no clear sense of a way forward.

From that afternoon, and for the next month, I thought of any and every way I could to keep my baby. But the days marched on, and I grew bigger. The delivery would happen... soon... and what was I going to do?

I imagined every possible scenario. Moving back in with my parents temporarily was a solution if I lived. But would they accept me and my baby under these circumstances? I seriously doubted it.

Who would care for the baby when I went to work, which I would have to do to survive. If I died, what would happen to the baby. The thought of my baby in a series of foster homes was unacceptable...I had been taught the importance of an infant's need to bond, immediately after birth, with its mother. And I believed that as long as there was a permanent 'mother' to bond with, the infant would feel secure....

Years later, as I worked in the field of adoption, I

found that there was often significant trauma to an infant when it was separated from its natural/birth mother right after birth.

Further, I did not believe my parents would accept a child conceived and born out of wedlock, and since none of my younger siblings were able to accept the responsibility, I had to forget any help coming from my family.

The more I thought about it, the more I realized I had no other options.

With only a week to go I found myself emotionally drained and physically exhausted. In the doctor's office that week, the subject of adoption was of utmost importance. With all options gone, I finally agreed to the adoption, knowing full well my decision had already been made for me.

It was the Fifties.

The obstetrician insisted that I not be awake during the delivery...that way I would not see the baby or even know its sex—"which," he told me, "will make it easier for you to forget this happened and get on with your life." I had no idea how untrue and impossible this would be.

Once the baby was delivered and arrangements were made for its care, I prayed that I would die. The toxemia was at a critical level and I did not want treatment, but the specialist called in had been a good friend of mine before the pregnancy and he gave orders for my immediate care.

And so my baby was taken in one direction... and I was taken in another.

Mercifully, the nurses put me in a non-obstetric ward. There I would not be around other mothers or hear the newborn babies cry.

Then something totally unexpected happened. Amid all the precautions to keep any identifying information from me, the pediatrician who checked all the newborns came into my room one day and asked for me by name. When I responded, he said, "You have a perfectly healthy baby girl. She weighs 6 pounds and 5 ounces and is taking formula well." Apparently, he was unaware the baby was to be adopted. I often wondered if a higher force had something to do with this slip.

He failed to tell me she had a full head of black, curly hair.

The effects of the toxemia did not resolve as they should have following delivery and I remained in the hospital an additional ten days. The baby could not be discharged until I was, so my doctors and the adopting parents were anxious for me to recover. The day before I was to be discharged, a nurse wheeled me into a conference room, where I was to sign the papers releasing the baby for adoption. I would be giving up all rights to see or contact her until she was 21. I felt weak and sick. My hands shook as I signed the document, and as I tried to look at the other signature on the paper the social worker yanked the pages from me.

"You cannot see that," she said angrily.

As I signed the document, giving custody of my child to people whose name I could not know, I felt her slip from my hands along with those pages.

Nothing I am ever asked to do in my whole life will be more difficult than this, I thought. *Nothing will ever be this painful.*

And in that moment I made a promise to my daughter.

When you are twenty-one and this document is no longer valid, I vowed, *I will find you.*

In April, 1977, twenty one years later, I gave birth to our fifth child, born to me and my then-husband, Charles. As I looked at my beautiful baby girl I remembered a promise I had etched on my heart long before to a baby girl I had been forbidden to see.

Within months, I began to search for her. The physician who delivered her and arranged the private adoption was the link to my child, so, I thought, it should not be too difficult. But when I contacted him, he told me, "I have no records or any recollection of your case. That was long ago."

He wanted me to go away and forget my child, but a mother never forgets.

My search was going to be more than difficult—soon I would see that it was going to be almost impossible. While I was discouraged, however, I was not defeated. I would have to find her without him. But where would my help come from?

In fact, my "help" would come from truly remarkable sources. For as I began to search for my daughter, I also found myself at the beginning of a spiritual journey—one that would lead me beyond the bounds of the traditional religion I had been raised with. Very soon I would find myself opened to a new world of the spirit. A world about which I was at first skeptical... and yet a world that eventually became more real to me than the concrete world I'd previously known.

My search for the truth had opened this new door and I walked through it, encountering the invisible world that exists all around us. As I followed its challenging path, I found myself being led on one of the most exciting and deeply rewarding journeys of my life....

CHAPTER 1

AFTER MY FIRST BABY was born and taken away from me sight unseen, I needed to create a new life for myself. Not certain how or where I would do this I returned to Philadelphia where I was offered a job in the hospital where I had worked before.

As I went about my work, and returned to everyday life among old friends I tried to forget that I had carried and delivered a child. But that was impossible. I realized immediately that a mother can *never* forget. All she can do is try to move on with her life when her child is gone. I tucked away my promise to her, knowing that one day I would locate her and share with her the facts of her beginning.

But something else unusual happened to me, as well. The doctor told me the adopting parents were from out of state, but once I was back in Philadelphia, something strange kept occurring. I felt her presence. In fact, I felt it strongly. I knew she was in the area.

While it was difficult for me to let go emotionally, something else gave me a sense of hope and comfort.

The day I agreed to the adoption, I heard the doctor call his nurse into his office which was within earshot of the examining room where I was getting dressed. "Lucy," I overheard him say to her, "call Louise Thomas and tell her we have a good baby for her this time." Then he added, "both parents are professionals and in good health. The father is in his thirties and the mother in her twenties, the father is handsome, and the mother is very pretty."

I would *never, ever* forget the name, Louise Thomas. I wrongfully believed, back then, it was the name of the adopting mother who had at least one child and was waiting to adopt another one. After all, I had requested my child be placed in a home with siblings.

Now, back in the Philadelphia area, and drawn by an invisible magnet, I began to search for a Louise Thomas. I came up blank. At the time I had no way of knowing she was only the intermediary. I always believed that some day she would be the link to my daughter.

And so I was left with two forces at work in my life: One, an unusual sense that somehow I *would* one day find my child again—even if it meant waiting 21 years. And the other was the sense that, despite the empty spot in my heart, I was to go on and forge a new life for myself.

Far easier said than done.

Two months after the baby was born I met the man who I would eventually marry.

Now, with Charles in my life I began to feel better about myself. Soon our busy life took my mind off the baby, at least a bit. He began to court me, and I felt safe. We knew many of the same people and he was good company. I began to feel like a normal human being again, and not like a woman who was marked with the "scarlet letter" of shame.

I returned to my nursing career believing it would replace the constant thoughts of my child, and lift me out of my world of sadness. I found, however, that only time can lessen that kind of pain. Everywhere, I encountered painful reminders.

The next year I returned to Virginia and went to work in the OR of a large hospital, where I worked with a nurse who recently had a baby. She told us that her husband was an anesthesiologist, and mentioned the hospital where he worked. She was a quiet, lovely woman who rarely spoke of her life outside the OR. I not only enjoyed working with her, but felt an unusual closeness to her. Later, I found out that she did not have a husband but was an unwed mother who had the courage to keep her baby. At first I felt a twinge of jealousy and regret, because she *had* her baby and I did not. Then I found myself feeling sorry for her. The social stigma attached to being an unwed mother was forcing her to live a lie. At least I would not have to lie—but I knew that if I did not keep my mouth shut and bury the truth there would be severe social consequences.

Another time, when assigned to the maternity ward, I carried a baby to its mother on the morning she was being discharged. I handed her the baby, then busied myself in the room as she dressed her baby. When finished, she wrapped the infant in a small blanket, cradled it close to her and kissed it. Instead of looking happy, as I'd expected, she had a very sad expression on her face. I left the room, wondering.

When I mentioned this to the Head Nurse, she said, confidentially, "She is an unmarried attorney who is giving her baby up for adoption. She felt that if she dressed the baby herself and handed it to the intermediary, she would not feel as though she was abandoning it."

I felt anguish for the young mother. Her heart must be tearing in two. Many years later I realized how healing her actions were. But I also knew my physician had been right. If I had ever laid eyes on my own baby I would never have been able to give her up.

And there was an uncanny circumstance, as well. As

if something did not *want* me to forget.

Shortly after my new relationship began, I was introduced to a close friend and colleague of Charles who was an obstetrician with a large family. The first time I walked into their home, the man's wife handed me their baby. I soon learned—much to my shock—that this child was born on the same day as my baby. I knew this was not my baby, but the "coincidence" was just too strange to ignore.

Charles and I spent many evenings with these friends, and at first I found it too painful to be around this child. Every cry, every new gesture, every smile and coo, reminded me that my arms were empty. And yet that strange feeling would return, the one that told me my baby and I were—despite the physical separation—somehow strongly, invisibly connected. And as the months passed and I watched this little one develop I felt the invisible connection to my own baby grow stronger. For one thing, on a practical level, by observing this child, I could tell when my little one was starting to smile, cut teeth, crawl, sit up, walk, and say her first words.

As she grew, the toddler would often run to me and climb up on my lap. Through this child, I was able to follow my own child's growth, and hopefully her development.

And so, inwardly, I found myself marking time by the ages of my daughter and what she must be doing at that time. I wondered if other adoptive mothers did the same thing. But I was not aware of any other mothers who had given up a child. Only years later would I find that I was not the only birth mother who felt a part of her was missing, an inner sense of loss, even when she had other children. It was universal.

When my daughter was four....

I married Charles. Accepted by his friends, and the fact that we seemed to be compatible, I felt good about the marriage. I wanted a respectable life with a family, and marriage would bring that. The fact that we married out of the Church (Charles was divorced), did not seem as serious a sin as the one I had previously committed.

Regardless of the rules we broke, I still felt married. And regardless of the fact that the Church considered my child illegitimate, I most certainly did not.

She was perfect. Beautiful. Mine.

And one day, no matter what it took, I would find her.

CHAPTER 2
(RULES)

FOR THE THREE YEARS before Charles and I were married I had been graciously accepted into his family. They had a difficult time understanding my parents' negative behavior to my relationship with Charles. But when we told his family we planned to get married in a civil ceremony, they bristled.

"And what are you going to do about the Church?" they asked. We realized we had a problem reconciling our faith with the rules forbidding a divorced person from re-marrying, but assured them we felt confident the Church would be more helpful once we were married.

We delayed our marriage, hoping that Charles' annulment to his first marriage would go through. He wrote letters, spoke with numerous Church authorities, and went to great lengths so we could be married in the Church. All without resolution.

When I mentioned our plans to some of my friends, one of them warned me. "God will punish you if you do this." She was a very religious person who followed the Church's rules to the letter.

My family totally turned their backs on us. "You will not be welcome in our home if you marry out of the Church." They did not attend the marriage and we were never in my parent's home again, so rigid was their belief system.

Despite these warnings and threats, we were married by a judge at City Hall in Philadelphia June 28, 1960. My sister Joan was the only family member to attend. Another sister, Mary, would have come, but she had just had a baby. None of Charles' family was present.

While marrying outside the Church bothered me, something else was going on inside my head. I had not broken up a marriage, since Charles was divorced before I met him. In my eyes, he was free. I continued to believe that the Church would eventually allow us back in its good graces once we established ourselves as a family, attended Mass, raised our children as Catholics—and keep our civil marriage a secret.

Perhaps it was the Church's hard line toward us, and feeling pushed away from a church to which I'd been faithful my whole life, but suddenly I gained a sort of outsider's perspective. For starters, it amazed me how a Church that represented God's love and forgiveness could so suddenly turn on its heel and show the face of anger and rejection the moment you didn't, or couldn't, live by its rules.

I soon began to question many rules that had been ingrained into my head most of my life. I began to wonder if anyone was really in Hell because they ate meat on Friday.

I re-read scripture, wondering how many church rules actually came from God. How many were man made, written to hold together the diverse followers of Christ in the early Church. Guidelines for an era that no longer existed.

As our marriage began to take shape, and we integrated ourselves into the medical and social community, I felt as married as any other couple. While we were still excluded from my family, Charles' family was the opposite. They put our civil marriage aside and considered us 'married.' We attended Mass when we visited them but did not go to communion. No one ever mentioned the Church...until....

Charles' niece was to be married and I was asked to be one of her attendants. "You know you can't receive communion at the wedding," I was told.

Sure enough, the priest, having been forewarned, passed me by when he distributed communion to the wedding party. Once again the message was clear. *You have not followed the rules, therefore you are not worthy of grace.*

I thought, *This is not right.*

Even though my mind told me these actions were wrong, my old feelings of shame and guilt were once again stirred up.

Vaguely, the idea began to surface. The Church is so much about rules. Rules that bring shame and guilt rather than a compassionate understanding of life. My father had gone way beyond the Church in his treatment of us, his children, and added his own rules. Most likely he believed it was necessary in order to bring home a point. It did more than that. It had damaged my spirit. So far, I had lived my life trying to stay within the framework of someone else's rules —rules that, frankly, did not make sense.

That little incident of not being allowed to receive Communion, even as a member of the wedding party, seemed to be more a lesson to others who might break a rule than a logical consequence of my action. *Do what you are instructed, or be denied God's grace.*

From that time I found myself beginning to question just about everything. And as I questioned, I began to realize that my "unaccepted" status within my family of origin was not totally my own doing.

When I thought about my life experience I realized, for instance, that no one had prepared me to be a sexually mature adult. We were given a litany of rules, and a list of don'ts. Educated by nuns in grade school, high school, and at Georgetown, little of anything was taught on the subject of sexuality or how to protect yourself. The message was: *Just do not have sex.* A girl usually found out on her own. Sex was a forbidden. Period.

If I had questions, there was no one to ask. The truth came only from the Church, and my parents and teachers were under Her guidance. Anything outside the lines was not acceptable... and I was not acceptable because I went outside those lines.

First, my unwed pregnancy brought shame to the family. Guided by the Church, they could not allow me in their home. Now, this second transgression, my *marrying* out of the Church, put them in yet another compromising situation.

It was not possible for me to have a good image of myself under these conditions.

And so I'd felt constantly torn between what seemed right, and what others thought was right.

It would be years before I felt anger toward those who should have taught rather than repressed information that a young woman needed in her world of sexuality.

Only when I confronted these issues, learned to forgive myself, and connected to the God I thought had abandoned me, was I able to function as a totally integrated being.

But that came much later.

I would come to see that, over the centuries as the hierarchy of the Church grew, and She become wealthy, She not only lost touch with the people, but created even more rules. The basic teachings of Christ...to love one another...had been divested of its meaning, as evidenced by the treatment of those born with a different sexual orientation.

Pope John XXIII tried to bring the outdated Church to modern times. He preached openness and responsibility for our own soul, but his untimely death sent the Church back into the Middle Ages.

I would witness upheaval, and see many leaving the Church, not because they wanted to, but because hidden behind its rules, it is not hearing the people. Of course there are groups within the Church who feel their eternal salvation is secure if they just follow the rules and never seek or question. But they are not the Church, only a segment of it.

I would discover I was not one of those people, I preferred to follow this teaching of God, found in scripture. In John 13, verse 34-35, "A new command I give you; Love one another, as I have loved you." This is the law that led me to the path I took in my search for my daughter... the law that also allowed me to doubt and question much of what I had been taught. And as I began to search for her, I found something else. A spirituality that embraced

God in His fullness, not only through music and in the cathedrals where we worship Him, but even more so in the beauty of His creation, in nature.

In the stillness of an evening; beside the sea; looking out the window of a plane; walking on soft grass; on a mountaintop; sometimes I would visit the grave of a friend or relative who served our country, in Arlington National Cemetery near my home in suburban Washington DC. This was where I found God. God was beside each and every soul whose body had been laid to rest on those hollowed grounds regardless of race or nationality or religious belief.

Those are the places where I felt His peace, where He wiped my tears, answered my prayers, showed me I could be happy when in pain. Because He is everywhere. How did I reconcile my relationship with Him then, if I was also supposed to accept rules imposed on me which seemed to contradict so much of what He came to teach us?

To find the answers, I had to search deeply into my faith and found that I began to grow beyond what I was taught. "Seek and you will find," "Knock and the doors will be opened to you," "Ask and you shall receive."

I would indeed find new doors swinging open.

So began an incredible journey....

CHAPTER 3
(FORGING A NEW LIFE)

I FOUND THAT BEING so close to the two people I loved and lost, was taking its toll on me, so I left Philadelphia. I had begun to date Charles and, with some strong encouragement from him, I returned to Virginia where I had no trouble finding a position in nursing.

I moved into an apartment near the hospital and began to feel better about myself. Within a year, I was offered a much better position elsewhere and moved to a more convenient location. I was thankful for these changes that were taking place in my life. They kept me occupied, and diverted my mind from the sad events of the past.

Now, I was a married outcast from my own religion. We purchased a new home in McLean, Virginia and were expecting our first baby.

While there were plenty of distractions, I still found myself thinking of my other baby frequently. As much as I tried to put it all behind me, there would always be triggers to remind me of her existence, such as the friends' baby born on the same day.

During the pregnancy with our first child, the memory of my earlier pregnancy would often surface, and I would begin to feel once again, the sadness and remorse of the prior years. I knew I had to put those memories aside, and concentrate on the new baby I was about to deliver, but it was difficult.

As my due date approached, I was filled with an imaginary high. I envisioned an easy, normal delivery, with my husband by my side, both of us anxiously waiting to see if it was a boy or a girl, since sonograms were not available back then.

My husband told me to be *sure* I was in labor before he took me to the hospital. It would be embarrassing for a physician to bring his wife to the hospital in false labor. With the previous pregnancy, I was induced, had a brief, quick labor and was put to sleep for the delivery, so really had no normal labor to compare this with.

My husband's warning, plus my erratic contractions, which were nowhere near the usual signs of labor; (regular contractions, lasting one minute, occurring less than ten minutes apart), caused me to wait too long. I arrived at the hospital ready to deliver.

It was too late for regional anesthesia, and since I insisted on being awake, delivered naturally, enduring a painful delivery as anyone in earshot could tell.

My whole concentration was centered on seeing the baby and knowing its sex. When the doctor showed me my beautiful, blonde baby girl, I burst into tears. Seeing Cara triggered the memory of delivering another baby girl that I never saw, and I could not stop crying.

From within, the sense of loss tormented me. *How could I ever have given up my own flesh and blood!*

As they wheeled me from the delivery suite to my room, I could not quiet the emotions that had resurfaced from my previous delivery. Both Charles and the obstetrician assumed my emotional state was due to the trauma and pain of the delivery.

"I'm so sorry, Nancy," the doctor said. "We'll give you some Demerol in just a few minutes for the pain and you'll feel much better."

"There is no amount of Demerol that can help this kind of pain," I told him.

We can bury something just so deep but even without triggers I knew I would never be able to put the other child out of my mind. My only hope was that the pain of loss would lessen with time.

One year later, Matthew was born, and two years after that, Jeffrey. Thankfully, I seemed to be less emotional when the boys were born. Now, I had little time to dwell on the past. I had three children under three, and a husband who—it was turning out—was most uncooperative.

I have written about this elsewhere, but as the family grew, my husband became more difficult and unpleasant due to the added responsibilities and accompanying expense. He became abusive and this pushed me more deeply into a reliance on spirituality as I tried to reconcile my life with God's will.

We continued to see our friends whose little girl shared my child's birthday, and now, busy with my own family, I found I was a lot less emotional than before when around her. Yet, her birthday—August 1, was always a reminder and I would try to be careful about letting my emotions show, especially as the children grew and became aware if I seemed sad or distracted. Once I heard Cara, our three- year- old, say to her father, "Mommy's been crying today. Are you mad at her?" It was my other daughter's eighth birthday. Even then, I would look at my own children and wonder if *she* was as happy and loved.

Since I could not send her a present, I went to Mass every year on her birthday.

Before we had children, Charles and I would go to the Jersey shore several times a year for long week-ends. Once we had children, the children and I would stay for the month, and Charles would come up on week-ends. It really was not a vacation in the beginning, as I had no help with the children who needed constant supervision especially when near the water, which they all loved.

Eventually, we began to bring a sitter with us and continued to do so until the kids got older. The summers at the shore were very special to me. Having a sitter enabled me to take my early morning walk along the water's edge and then on the beach later during the day while the children were napping. I loved to walk the beach, but preferred to walk alone...This need grew stronger over the years because it was here in the quiet, by the sea, that I communicated with my "Summer Child," which is what I began to call her. For it was in the summer and at the seashore that I felt her presence more and would 'talk 'to her there.

Somehow, I just felt her nearby. In those walks by the sea, she was real to me and since I could not talk to her, I "wrote" letters to her as I walked along the sand. Letters filled with things I wanted to say to her, things I felt she needed to know, such as how awful I felt about her being adopted. Obviously, I could not mail these letters to her, but I needed to "write" them anyway...it connected me to her. So, I continued to write and then just store them in my head.

Along these walks, I would often stop when I saw a little child playing on the sand. Always looking for a blonde, blue eyed, little girl that resembled me. (I assumed she had my coloring, the other children did, even though my husband had dark brown hair and brown eyes.) I would ask the parents where they lived...and something about the little girl, trying to determine if the child was adopted.

Every summer as time passed, I looked for her along the beach, so near to where she had been born, because she was there. I *knew* she was.

By now I had come into touch with an uncanny sense that was growing in me—one to which I'd slowly learn to pay attention.

Back home, life began to evolve around the children's school and activities, leaving little time for quiet reflection those days.

When Cara, our first born, was in second grade she would make her First Communion at Marymount, a Catholic girls school, rather than at Holy Trinity, our parish in Georgetown. It bothered me greatly that I would not be allowed to receive communion with her and I wanted to talk to our pastor, Father Gavigan, about this.

I had often spoken with Fr. Gavigan about other issues and we were good friends.

That day I was upset as I told him how badly I felt about not being allowed to receive Communion at our daughter's First Communion. He looked at me and said. "You are in a real marriage, raising the children Catholic, and *wanted* to marry in the Church. You should be allowed to receive the sacraments. "

"A parish priest has the authority to grant a dispensation from some church rules and I am giving you that dispensation." He suggested Charles and I continue to attend Holy Trinity rather than the parish where we lived in Virginia, so as not to be a so- called "bad example"—the Church's term for those who don't live by the rules—in case some parishioners were aware of our civil marriage. "You don't want to violate someone else's religious sensibilities," he said, wisely, "while acting in good conscience about your own."

He then led me into the sacristy, and up to the main altar of the Church, where I received Holy Communion for the first time in eight years.

Cara's First Communion Day was a celebration for all of us, including my mother who also was present.

My father had died five years before, and now that she was no longer under his rule, had become a part of our family and no longer hung up on our "sinful" marriage. Life was as it was supposed to be.

From these experiences I saw how quickly the rules evaporate. And how long grace and love endure.

CHAPTER 4
(A NEW SPIRTUALITY)

ACCEPTED BACK INTO the Church—albeit quietly and with no fanfare—I began to wonder how many other rules had forced good people into sacrificial and painful lives. Now, I felt like I was back home, and my pathway to communication with God was once again open.

And did I ever want to talk to Him!

I had many questions that sought answers. My interest in the metaphysical world had been tweaked by books I had recently read by Ruth Montgomery, a nationally syndicated news columnist, who often appeared in the Washington Post. In the mid Sixties, she wrote *A Gift Of Prophesy*, a book about the life and prophesies of the famed psychic, Jeanne Dixon who was married to a well- known businessman in Washington, DC. I felt an intense desire to meet or talk to Jeanne Dixon.

Jeanne had predicted the assassination of President John F. Kennedy in Dallas seven years before it happened, and had often given Ruth information for her columns. But it was not the predictions that interested me as much as the other material Ruth wrote about. A Christian, she often mentioned *the world beyond, the many lives we have lived, and the invisible world* around us in the ten other books she wrote after *A Gift Of Prophesy*.

Ruth Montgomery was a woman with excellent credentials. As a reporter, she'd covered Presidents and First Ladies for twenty –five years. I could not easily dismiss her work as anything but factual.

What I read made sense to me and I wanted to know more about that invisible world she spoke of. Where Ruth wrote about these events, Jeanne practiced her psychic profession openly. Here was a well- known Catholic woman doing something we were told was *a sin, and the Church had not silenced her*. I needed to talk to Father Gavigan.

"Why are you so interested in this phenomenon?" he asked.

"I really don't know," I said. I didn't mention the uncanny and powerful presence of my child I felt every year at the seashore. "I just want to know more about it. I feel there is so much more to life than we know, and the subject fascinates me. "

"Read Edgar Cayce," he told me. Cayce, known as the "sleeping prophet" from Virginia Beach, Virginia, had died in the Thirties. I had never heard of him but subsequently purchased all the books I could find on him and his prophetic insights—all delivered while he was in trances, and most extremely accurate. Through the readings and other books they led me to, I found that there were metaphysical laws that applied, whether we understood them or not. Those laws teach us why things are the way they are.

It was my introduction to a more open-minded spirituality.

Fr. Gavigan and I had many conversations over the years, and not once did he rebuke me for my interest in the other spiritual world. In fact, he encouraged me to explore it. "We don't have all the answers," he told me.

And so this wonderful, holy man gave me permission to further explore a world I wanted to better understand. He opened the door to broader possibilities, and through my readings I realized I had already experienced my own introduction to spiritual phenomena—I just had not recognized them for what they were.

As a young girl I'd had an active imagination, and often said things that got me in trouble because they just "came out." Sometimes I would ask myself, "Why did I say that?" In grade school, I once told my best friend that I was going to be a nurse, marry a doctor and have five children. Later, as a young nurse, I was told by the chief of obstetrics that I would probably never be able to have children, so I should prepare myself.

Years later, of course, I'd married Charles—a physician—and we had five children.

Once, while in high school, I came home to find my mother sitting at the dining room table chatting with her close friend and neighbor. They were trying to convince me to go to the school's Senior prom with her son, Joe.

"He's too intelligent for me," I said. "He speaks to me in Latin and Greek and I can't understand what he's saying." But even as we focused on the prom, something else was nagging at me. I sensed Mom's friend was pregnant. Wanting to change the subject, I said to her, "I forget, Mrs. L., how many children do you have now?"

"Five," she said, and giving my mother a rather unfriendly look, got up and, shortly, left to go back home.

My mother was furious. "What made you say that to her?" she screamed at me. "She told me in strict confidence that she was pregnant, but did not want anyone to know until she was further along. Who told you she was pregnant?"

"No one," I said, uneasily. "I just had a feeling she was pregnant."

This was not the first or last time I was made to feel wrong and intrusive about my "knowings" and started to keep them mostly to myself.

Not too long after the incident with Mrs. L. I found myself alone in the house, washing dishes. This was a rarity as there were ten of us in the family. Suddenly, I "saw" my beloved Uncle Jack dead. He was the delight of our lives, especially mine. Uncle Jack had recently been discharged from the Marines, and was a healthy, handsome 47 year-old man. I adored not only him, but Kathryn, his companion. When I saw him dead, in my mind's-eye, I cried so intensely I could not stop—the mere thought of him dying was that overwhelming. I was glad no one was home, I could never have told them why I was crying.

Several months later, when Joe brought me home from his Senior Prom, my father was waiting inside. I could tell from the way he looked that something was wrong. Dad put his arm around me and his words were like a knife in my heart: "Uncle Jack died tonight from a heart attack."

Brokenhearted and sad beyond belief, I could not tell anyone the truth. I truly believed in the secrecy of my own heart that I caused his death. He was far too young to die naturally. It was years before I was able to accept the fact that I had not caused his death by my thoughts, but had simply been intuitive.

There were other instances where I just seemed to know things, and at the time it was frightening. The truth is that as I got older, these incidents had continued and grown more striking.

Once, as a visiting nurse, I was on my way back to the main office at the end of the day when I thought I'd make one more house call. I pulled up in front of the patient's home, but did not get out. Instead, I turned the car around and headed for the Sousa Bridge and drove back into DC. Halfway across the bridge, I felt something had happened to my father. He was temporarily working in Mobile Alabama, and my mother was at home in Virginia.

I was still *persona non grata* with the family, because of the unwed pregnancy, and not sure if anyone would call to let me know if anything was wrong. The feeling was so strong that I was determined to call them and ask about my father's wellbeing.

The red light flashing on the phone as I opened my door told me something was amiss. I played back the recording and heard my mother's voice. "I just want to let you know your father had a heart attack this afternoon. He is in the hospital and they say he'll be alright, but I am going down there." It happened an hour before —as I was crossing the Sousa bridge.

While I knew I had not caused *his* heart attack, I was still years away from fully recognizing the phenomena that had become a part of my life.

Still, the incidents continued.

Some years after my father's heart attack, I was

shopping for clothes for the three children one day, when I had an overwhelming sense of disaster. I put the items down on the counter at Garfinckle's and told the salesperson I would be right back. I raced to the payphone and called home.

Vernell, our beloved housekeeper, answered the phone. The poor woman was frantic. "I couldn't reach Dr. Hannan because he's playing golf and I knew you were not due home for a couple hours." Then the story spilled out.

Our four year old, Jeff, while attempting to slide down the two-story bannister, had fallen over the railing and landed on the slate floor. He was bleeding from his head and his arm hurt.

I told Vernell what to do until I got home, and instructed her to contact the club and tell them to have Dr. Hannan come home right away. Then I flew out of the store without the clothing and headed home, praying Jeff would be all right.

We took him to the hospital where they set his broken arm and sutured his bleeding scalp. Mercifully, he was not more seriously injured, and the children were reminded of the consequences of giving in to the temptation of the forbidden bannister.

Exactly ten years later, I experienced something uncannily similar. Again, shopping for the kids' clothes, I felt an uneasiness that lingered. No panic like last time, just a feeling that something was not right. When it did not go away, I put the clothes down, as before and just drove on home.

I had no sooner walked in the door when I heard the crying. The sitter was running to the hall where our son, Jon had just fallen. I was there to pick him up and was able to take him to the hospital right away.

In another strange twist, Jon was also four—the same age as Jeff when he fell in the same manner, breaking the same bone and incurring a similar cut on his head.

These "knowings" were not confined to major events. They seemed to pervade my life.

More than once during those years when the children were small, I would simply know when the sitter who came every Tuesday and Thursday, was not coming—but in a strange way. Someone would invariably call on either day, knowing I had a sitter and ask me to go somewhere or do something with her. Without hesitating, I would reply, "Sorry, I can't go, my sitter can't make it today." I had no knowledge that was true at the moment, but the words would just… come out.

Moments later, I would get the call from the sitter. "Mrs. Hannan, I can't come in today…," and offer the reason.

And now, with Fr. Gavigan's encouragement, I actually opened the door to something I'd been ignoring, minimizing, and dismissing.

After years of hearing a loud knock on the door, only to find no one was there; or hearing my name called; or experiencing recurring dreams that seemed to have a meaning, I felt that maybe I was on my way to learning the truth about all these uncanny happenings.

I began to wonder, *Is there more to life than what we see? Are the mysterious events that happen to us somehow linked to the spiritual world? How real is that world—or is it my imagination? And if it's real, is it a source of good?*

I did not know. I only knew I had to find out.

CHAPTER 5

WITH THE BIRTH of each child, my life became busier and I had less time to dwell on the future. My daughter would be in grade school now, and I eagerly anticipated the day when she would reach twenty-one and I could initiate my search for her. Until then, I put the logistics of how to find her on-hold. After all, I reasoned, it would be a simple matter of asking the doctor who delivered her and who facilitated the adoption, to forward the letter I would write her at the proper time in the future. Since the adoptive mother had presumably been a patient of his, he would know how to get in touch with the family. And so, with that plan tucked away in my heart, I was able to concentrate on my growing family.

By anyone's standards, my children and I lived

comfortably. Charles and I eventually built a larger home to accommodate our growing family and frequent house guests, mostly my in-laws. I enjoyed entertaining our friends and the new house made it even more enjoyable. I looked forward to the month at the Jersey shore with the children and with my husband coming up on week-ends. In addition, he and I would travel to medical meetings several times a year, always held at an upscale golf resort.

The children were good students and caused us little worry outside of the minor growing pains of childhood and teen years. I did not work during the marriage, but stayed home to run the house and raise the children. While I limited most of my outside activities to the children's schools I did accept some social responsibilities relating to my husband's profession.

While life seemed to be on a normal course, it was anything but normal. Though I was financially secure and comfortable, I was not happy. Something major was missing in this marriage. The absence of intimacy and productive communication were obvious. But it was the not-so-obvious that concerned me as I attempted to unravel the unknown.

Elsewhere I have written about the abusive marriage in which I remained for far too long, for what seemed like good reasons at the time. What I did not include in that story of eventual escape from abuse was the way my intuitive side deepened as my plan to locate my daughter one day budded and my interest in things spiritual broadened and deepened.

For instance, I would look at other marriages to see what held them together, and in the process, found that I was, in fact, becoming much more intuitive. I could look at a couple and tell if they were happy, or just pretending to be. I could sense discord, something amiss or deeper problems just by seeing how they interacted.

While I never mentioned my observations to anyone, I was invariably, proven right.

In this way, the experience of having left a part of me behind was changing me in several ways. I found myself studying people. Always looking beyond the obvious.

Always looking for answers...Always looking for a blonde, blue-eyed little girl.

I made my first steps into the intuitive world slowly, not realizing that over time it would become much more important in my life and, eventually, even in my search.

In my outer world, all the comforts of our good life did not prevent the marriage from slowly decaying from the inside and disintegrating. While I began to notice the subtle changes in my husband, I chalked them up to additional responsibility with the growing family, which was his most vocal nuance.

When I was pregnant with our fourth child I saw a dramatic change in him. He became much more belligerent, angry, argumentative—and for the first time, physically abusive, not only to me but to the children.

He constantly accused me of infidelity. If it had not been so hurtful, it would have been comical. He watched my every move. When in the world would I have had time to escape to a love nest? Something was going on with Charles, and I still did not get it.

I noticed other changes, as well. His drinking escalated. His patterns of behavior changed. His attachment to male friends outside of the family became deeper. I had strong feelings there was a woman in his life as well.

I sensed these things, as my intuitive side grew. But still, I did not see fully the pattern that was evolving and which would eventually result in the end of my marriage.

Maybe because my outer life was slowly unraveling, and most definitely because I felt an inward tug, I continued to search for answers in the world of spirituality. *Where was the meaning in my life? Was it simply to bear and raise children? Was I supposed to tolerate demeaning behavior, and if so, why? Am I being punished for* my *long ago "sins"?* I prayed to God almost constantly. I read in order to learn, and to find the answers. And they often came to me in a manner I least expected.

As life gradually became more unpleasant and my husband distanced himself from me both physically and emotionally, I felt abandoned. Both by him, and by God. My prayers were not being answered, or so I thought, and I wondered if they were even heard.

But I *was* hearing something, or someone, during those years. The Seventies were the most active, probably because by that time I had begun to look into the spiritual world through different lens. I needed to understand what was going on around me.

Often, I would hear my name called loud and clear... sometimes when no one was at home. Many times, I answered knocks on the door, only to find the "prankster" was nowhere in sight.

During a particular period of time, another strange thing began happening. On several occasions I heard someone call out—*"Mother!"*—and would run to see who it was, believing it was one of my children. But then I would stop. This was not a voice I knew. And besides that, my kids always called me "Mom."

One night I was awakened, again, by one of the children calling to me from outside our bedroom door. "Mother, mother!" Too tired to get up, I called back, "Come on in, it's ok."

No one came in, so I got up and went out to the hall. No one was there, and when I checked on the children, they were all asleep.

These calls for "Mother" continued over a period of months, and I began to think something was wrong with me. They eventually stopped, and I forgot about them.

And then there was the recurring dream. I did not understand it. There would be a row of babies, lined up and crying. And then, one in the middle would appear to be an adult. It was saying to me over and over, "You didn't let me die. You didn't let me die." This baby I always dreamed about had a full head of black curly hair…maybe that is why I did not connect the dots, my other two girls had blond hair.

As things like this continued to occur, I only searched deeper.

My quest for answers led me to the metaphysical, and I began taking classes to better understand this new world I was interested in.

One of the first classes I attended was taught by Anne Gehman, a woman who was both a psychic and a medium and had recently moved to our area. She was soft-spoken, delightful, warm, and obviously knowledgeable. She seemed quite normal compared to a few psychics I had been run into earlier. I wanted to know more about this lovely woman. Hopefully, she would help diminish some of my skepticism. I was still resistant to the idea that psychics were valid when I started her classes, but soon found that all psychics were not the same.

In these classes, I began to understand more of our unseen world. I was intrigued to find that the answers I was looking for were so simple. Apparently, someone *was* trying to communicate with me, but *who*? And *about what*?

I was confused because I thought only the dead tried to contact the living.

For one thing, I learned this: When we pick up messages and intuitions it does not have to be a soul "on the other side" trying to contact us. It can be a living person, who desperately needs to communicate, sending out a strong resonance. Of those who have passed, I learned that they are of a higher vibration, and though we cannot see them they can contact us through our energy field.

All this flew in the face of the traditional religious upbringing, but I could not ignore or deny the reality of what I was experiencing.

As more and more unexplained events occurred, I continued to delve deeper. Anne had started me on a quest for knowledge of the unseen world, and eventually she would show proof of life-after-death in her work as a Medium. I needed no proof; it was something I just believed.

But it would take almost ten years for me to personally benefit from her gift. By then I would be comfortable with our unseen world, because I was coming to accept the unusual happenings in my life as normal.

Anne moved on to start her Spiritualist Church and I lost track of her for a few years. But since she had introduced me to this world, I continued to explore it with others, hoping to find more answers to my many questions.

In July 1976, we were back at the Jersey Shore, where I felt very close to my "Summer Child." Jon, our youngest, was now six and would be going into first grade. With all the children now in school, I would have the time to accomplish tasks I needed to do. These annual visits were like markers in my life, and I realized that the following summer, which would be August 1977, my daughter would be twenty-one and I could send my letter to her—the one I had carefully thought out for years.

But another major issue was facing me, and I had to take stock of my life and its direction.

In the fall, with the children all in school, I would be free to work at least part time if I had to, because I was ready to talk to an attorney about divorce. The marriage no longer existed. It had become a sham. His loyalty was elsewhere, I did not matter, and the physical abuse had escalated to a point that on occasion I feared for my life.

How I would manage was unclear, but fortunately, I had kept my RN license current, and finding a job should not be a problem. With all of those thoughts on my mind that summer, I still managed to enjoy the sun, ocean and temporary peace.

The day after we returned home from the shore, however, I went to visit my close friend, Kay, hoping she could shed some light on my miserable, confusing life. Kay was a lovely, well-bred Russian lady. She was also a gifted psychic. A mutual friend had introduced us several years before, and Kay and I developed a warm and supportive relationship. I recognized her psychic gift the first time we met, and finally convinced her to use it to help others.

Kay soon developed a high-level clientele, among whom was Imelda Marcos from the Philippines. On one of her visits to the States, Kay told Imelda that her husband would eventually be deposed, be forced to move to another country, where he would die in exile.

All this, famously, came to pass. So when Kay said something to me, I listened.

That day, sitting at her kitchen table, I begged her to tell me anything that would help me understand my unhappy life. "Kay, I need to know what's going on. I can't put my finger on it, but I need to know what I'm dealing with."

She looked at me for a moment, then looked away as though she was trying to decide what to say. "I don't want to hurt you," she said, "and if I tell you what I see, it will hurt you. But since you are so miserable and really want to know I'll tell you."

"And don't leave anything out," I replied, "I can handle it."

Reluctantly, Kay described a woman, several locations, and a type of behavior that was hard for me to accept.

Hurt, yes. Betrayed, definitely. But it made sense of so much of the past two years I actually felt relieved.

I knew Kay felt bad for revealing knowledge that hurt

me and I wanted to reassure her that her revelations had actually helped. I felt a weight lifted off me. "Of course I'm hurt and angry, but I no longer feel I'm to blame for his erratic behavior. Somehow, just having that information is a relief. Wondering was worse."

At least, I now had the ammunition I needed to confront him.

I thanked her and got up to leave. "Need to get home and start packing," I said. Kay hesitated for a moment before getting up and I sensed there was something else.

"Let's go outside," she said, "walls have ears." As if what I just heard wasn't enough. She was very quiet as we walked along the tree- shaded sidewalk by her townhouse.

"Are you ok?" she asked. "Do you feel all right? "

"I'm just tired," I said.

"Packing, unpacking, repacking for our trip tomorrow to another damn Medical meeting. This time at least we're taking the children so I'll have someone to talk to on the trip."

Without looking at me directly, she said, "Do you know you are pregnant?"

I stopped dead in my tracks, looked right at her and said, "Kay, I am forty-five and besides, that is impossible! Charles has not touched me in over two years. How can this be?"

And then I remembered the day he had come to

the Jersey shore unannounced, mid-week, while I was having my period. He all but forced me to have sex with him. That was only two weeks ago.

We resumed walking. I was in a state of disbelief, but she was not quite finished.

"The baby is a *girl*" she said, shaking her head, *"and a clone of you*! I'll have my hands full with *two* of you. She is coming to be with you, so you will not be alone, this baby is coming to help you."

Kay's words were not registering. She has to be wrong! Not now! I would "need her." She has come to "help"—Each of my children, —Cara, Matt, Jeff, and Jon—were a blessing and a joy and of course this child would be no different. *But how can a pregnancy help me at this time*, I thought. *How could this be happening? And now!*

I did not understand that unseen forces were already at work, showing me what I needed to do, while preventing me from initiating what would have been a disaster —which was to divorce Charles —at that particular time.

And this child conceived under such unusual circumstances was definitely meant to be, and not an accident. Divorce, at least at this time, was no longer an option. The search for my daughter would have to be side-lined.

My heart ached.

CHAPTER 6

THE FIRST THREE MONTHS of the new pregnancy were very upsetting. My obstetrician had insisted I consult a geneticist because of my age and the prospects of a Downs baby. The specialist was too negative for me and I disliked him, but went along with his recommended amniocentesis because of the possibility of a Downs baby. He had already told me that my "large uterine fibroids will grow along with the placenta, and eventually deprive the fetus of nourishment. We will do a Caesarean Section at seven months and keep the baby in an isolette where it can be fed artificially." And then he added, "IF you carry it that long."

I looked at the Geneticist and said, "Whatever happened to God? Doesn't He fit into the picture?" I never returned to see him, relying on the obstetrician who delivered the other children, and on my faith.

With only negatives, and no real encouragement, I wandered around in a mental fog. How could anything so awful happen to a child that was supposed to be? Kay had already told me the baby would be fine and not to worry, but I needed more validation.

And so, I trekked off to another psychic I knew. He was a very spiritual man and known for his accuracy. I said nothing to alert him to my condition or my anxiety about the baby's welfare.

The first thing he blurted out was, "I see you are pregnant, but there is a lot of anxiety round you. Why is that?"

I told him what the doctors had said. "Will the baby be all right?" I asked him.

"The baby is fine. It is a girl and she is perfectly healthy. I do not see any problems at all with the pregnancy and she will be delivered at term. This child will bring you much joy. Just be sure to get your proper nourishment, and rest when you get tired," he said..."*and stop harboring all the negatives.* There is no cause for alarm."

With that reassurance, I continued the pregnancy comfortable with the belief and knowledge that all would go well and I would deliver a healthy, full term baby. Once more, I had been reassured by forces from beyond.

Once reassured that the baby would be alright, I was free to deal with the rejection and hateful treatment that

Charles inflicted on me for the next nine months.

Adding to that was the hurtful validation that came from people who had no idea that their innocent remarks had struck a chord. His secret affairs were now well documented.

When Jenny was born that following April, I looked at my beautiful new baby and realized she had indeed come to show me what I needed to do.

The timing was perfect. In less than four months, her sister, the baby I was never allowed to see, would reach legal adulthood and the documents I signed long ago would no longer be valid. I not only had a right to know who my daughter was but had an obligation to share her history with her. Locating her should not take too long. All I had to do was mail a letter to my former obstetrician.

In the meantime, my attention settled on the new baby. She brought sunshine and joy to this unhappy family, and the other children cared for her needs as much as I did. Somehow, we managed to have her baptized at Holy Trinity without his objection.

While her father paid little attention to her, Matthew, who was now fifteen, bonded with her in his stead. He carried her everywhere. Once without my knowledge-— in fact I thought the baby was asleep in her crib-—he took her to an evening basketball game at Bishop O'Connell High School when she was only six months old!

Life was relatively quiet around the house those first

months of Jenny's life, mainly because Charles was rarely there, and when he was, he was not talking to me.

Undercover, I was doing my own thing. Caring for a new baby and driving car pools left little time for what I needed to do before our trip to the shore in July. I needed to track down my old obstetrician, compose the letter to both him and my daughter, and have the letter mailed before we left in July. This would set the stage for a reply by the time we returned back to McLean in August.

This was to be my summer of fulfillment. The moment I had waited for so long.

After I mailed the letter, I called the obstetrician to refresh his memory and let him know that the letter was on its way. I was not prepared for his response.

"Hello, Nancy," he said." Of course I remember you, how are you? Yes, I delivered you, but have no recollection of any adoption. I delivered many babies that were adopted, but for the sake of confidentiality, kept no records. When I retired, outdated records were destroyed. I am very sorry, I wish I could help you, but I can't."

Something inside me stirred. He was a well- respected and honest man, the Chief of Obstetrics in a major hospital. But he was lying. I put the receiver down, and tried to come to terms with what he had just said. He was protecting the adoptive parents. But he had also been my doctor, had arranged the adoption, and should have had some loyalty to me, but he didn't.

I knew very well that he remembered exactly who my baby had gone to.

I almost mentioned the name I had overheard in his office years before, but had a strong feeling that if he thought I knew their name, he would alert them, and they might disappear. I could not risk that right now.

I could still see him in my mind's-eye, even all these years later, sitting on the chair beside my hospital bed the morning he came in to discharge me. And I never forgot his words. "You are a very lucky woman," he said. "In all the years of my practice I have never seen a patient that close to death who did not die. Now, take some time to rest and your blood pressure should continue to come down. Get on with your life, and put this whole episode behind you."

He then suggested I move to Detroit, where he had already arranged a position for me in Henry Ford's Hospital. I would be far away from my child and her adoptive parents.

He had very clearly had a plan all worked out. And now, here I was, trying to undo it.

I'd thought the way forward would be easy.

Suddenly, it seemed impossible. Adoption records were sealed back then and only a Court Order would open them…it was wrongfully believed back then that a birth mother had no right to know the whereabouts or name of her child, even as an adult.

Yes, I may have forfeited my right to raise her, but I had not given away my right to know who she was.

I never even considered the reality that had just confronted me. It never occurred to me that my belief system was flawed. I only wanted to know who and where she was, allow her the opportunity to decide if she wanted to meet me. I wanted her to know the circumstances of her birth. And now, in one three-minute phone call, those dreams and hopes of twenty-one years had turned to ashes.

I needed to be back at the Shore, stand beside the ocean and talk to God. He would show me what to do. But that summer, we almost did not go. Still unable to accept the new baby, and still angry at me for "getting myself pregnant," Charles said we would not be going to the shore that summer. Only when he realized he had put a sizeable, non-refundable deposit on the house the previous summer did he renege.

And so, that summer we once again headed to the Jersey shore, but this year with a new baby who not only kept me distracted but happy. In fact, I marveled at this healthy baby. It was as if she were a sign from God.

I could see the other children splashing in the waves as I stood on the porch of the beach house, holding the baby in my arms, and I laughed to myself. I had felt such a strong energy from within to reject the doctors' opinion.

Uncharacteristically, I'd stood up to the geneticist when I asked him, "Whatever happened to God?"

I actually surprised myself when I blurted that out. And I never returned to him for future visits, but relied on the obstetrician who delivered the other children. And I relied on my steadily growing faith in the leading and power that came to me in spirit.

But the months of pregnancy had been a battle of faith for me. I'd found myself walking between the light of faith and courage and the darkness of doubt and fear.

When the dire prediction first came, Kay's words offered me a solid handrail to help me walk through the fear: *How could anything awful happen to a child that was* supposed *to be?* Light poured in, and I told myself, "What do doctors really *know*? They rely on what they are taught, and on statistical evidence—but where is their *faith*? Where is the hope I'm reaching for?" Kay had already told me the baby would be fine and not to worry.

On the other hand, fear had been present—like a shadow - and when I gave into it I'd sought more validation.

The psychic I had gone to gave me that validation, and the little girl in my arms was the sign... proof that forces from beyond were guiding me.

Still, the visible forces set against me finding

my first child were formidable. Could I walk in this growing assurance from the spiritual world that all would go well in my impossible search for her?

As the summer progressed, I wondered if there was anywhere else I could turn for help, now that the doctor was out of the picture. The only other person who had the information I needed was the attorney who handled the adoption. The very thought of him turned my stomach, but I would contact him anyway.

Avalon is close to Philadelphia, so I was able to locate a phone book with the Law firm's address and number. On a day I was alone, and the baby sleeping, I called his office. I discovered the attorney was deceased, but I spoke with the one who had bought the practice.

When I explained my situation, he advised me he would need a retainer of $10,000 just to look in the file, with no guarantee of any information. "You know," he spit out at me, "even though your documents are no longer valid, adoptions are closed and I would need the permission of the adoptive parents to give you any information." Obviously, I did not know that.

Flattened by his abrupt and callous delivery I said no thank you, and ended the conversation.

Now, there was literally, nowhere to turn.

Except one place, I would turn to God.

Further depressed by this recent phone call I wanted to go back to the ocean, walk on the beach and have my conversation with God, but it was now too close to dinnertime, and the children would be hungry. Not a good time to go. Besides, I needed the quiet of early morning for my encounter...and tomorrow I would have it.

The sun was just inching its way up over the horizon the next morning as I stood at the water's edge watching it come up. The surf was gentle, but invigorating as I stood in it, ankle deep. Not many vacationers were up and about this early and the few I had passed were farther up on the beach. I had God all to myself that morning.

Where is my daughter? The words cut into my heart.

I stared out into the sea, sensing a Presence I had not felt before. I could not think of what I wanted to say, I was so totally void of hope. I had five beautiful children still asleep one block away, yet, I had to find this other child of mine.

I looked past the sea and into the space beyond, and from the depths of my being, I spoke to God as I had never spoken to Him before. I did not gently ask Him for a favor, nor did I plead with Him, I ordered Him to help me.

"YOU HAVE TO HELP ME!" I pleaded. "THERE IS NO ONE ELSE! EITHER LEAD ME TO HER, OR HER BACK TO ME! YOU MUST! I HAVE NO ONE BUT YOU!"

I continued to stand in the water for a while, staring out into space. Filled with emotion and purpose, I told God I would do my part, if only I knew what it was.

Moments later, and with no desire to walk along the beach, I slowly walked through the sand and back to the house. Tears of anguish and despair fell down my cheeks and I just let the salt air dry them. But when I realized what I had just done, I told God I was sorry to have spoken to Him that way, and asked Him to forgive me for being so irreverent and disrespectful, for *ordering* Him to do something.

I suppose He forgave me, because I soon found out that God not only heard me, but had already set in motion a plan that began to slowly unfold. And when things got tough, I reminded myself that I had promised Him I would do my part.

Not knowing how difficult that would be.

CHAPTER 7

DURING THE EARLY Seventies, I had my first
psychic reading from a man named Sean Harribance.
My friend, Becky, who was very active in the Edgar
Cayce Foundation, invited me to her home one Saturday,
where Sean was doing readings for the few days he was
in Washington, DC, to visit relatives.

Sean had been studied by Duke University's para-
psychology department and found to be one of the more
accurate psychics they had encountered. With those credentials, I put my skepticism on hold and agreed to the
reading.

"He reads for fifteen minutes and talks fast," Becky
told me. "And he does not tape the reading, so try to
catch what he says." We walked down the hall to the
room where Sean would do the reading. "I'll be waiting

for you in the kitchen when you are finished," she added, "and don't be afraid, he's wonderful!"

I was met by a pleasant, stocky Jamaican, who had a kind, loving aura about him. I immediately felt comfortable in his presence, but had already decided I would be open to whatever he said, whether I agreed or not.

Without any preliminary introduction, he said, "You are in an unfulfilled marriage and it will never get any better. But, you are destined for three great loves in this life. You have had one, there will be two more.

"Did he mean 'loves' or marriages? I often wondered.

His next statement caused me to doubt his accuracy. "You are very close to God," he said.

I thought, *I wish that were true, but I am afraid I have broken too many commandments to be in His good graces right now.*

He spoke of the many levels in heaven, depending on our spiritual growth. I was fascinated by what he was saying because it made sense. And I wondered—if this was so, why didn't the Church teach us these things?

He moved on rapidly, telling me things about myself… and specifics about my childhood… so accurate in detail that I could not doubt that he had an extraordinary gift. He told me that some of the people in my life at the time had been connected to me in other lifetimes. In fact, he was specific about a certain person and told me how we were connected in a prior lifetime.

"He is here for awhile to help you through difficult times."

I knew who he was referring to. This man treated me with respect and dignity and I always felt uplifted when around him. He was easy to talk to and extremely observant. Don was a wonderful friend, a frequent guest in our home and an important influence in our boy's school. His uplifting manner often gave me the strength I needed to get through some of those times.

But now, we were suddenly on a vastly different turf.—*Other lifetimes? Connected in past lives?* Curious, I just listened.

As Sean brought up one lifetime after another, I was amazed to see how so much of who I was or what I did in a past life, directly related to this life. It was difficult to *not* believe him.

At one point in the reading, Sean digressed long enough to tell me that the moment I walked into the room it filled with so many images and scenes and people, he had a hard time selecting what to relate to me. "It feels like a giant movie screen that goes on and on," but said, I was "easy to read for," … whatever that meant.

"There is too much to tell you everything I see, so I tell you what I think is relevant."

When I thought he was finished, he had yet one more morsel of information for me. "You agreed to work through all of your karmas in this lifetime," he said. "That is why your life is so complicated. But, you will not have to come back again, unless you *choose* to."

Sean had just planted another seed. I *chose* to work through all my karmas? May *choose* to come back?

One day, I would understand what he was referring to, but back then, the concept was foreign to me.

My fifteen-minute reading lasted over one hour. I tried to remember all he said, and wrote most of it down later. But some things I was reluctant to tell my husband, so kept them to myself. Many times over the years, I would remember that reading, especially when something happened to validate what he had told me.

I had now been indoctrinated into this world of the spirit by two authentic psychics, but I still had serious doubts regarding this 'past lives' business.

I researched sacred scripture, looking for reference to having lived before, and I spoke with a Theologian friend about it as well. He pointed out that Saint Augustine, St. Clement, Origen and even Jesus taught about souls passing through various lives.

As amazing as it seems, it was sacred scripture that alluded to the fact we have lived here before, returning for the purpose of soul growth.

There are, for example, many chapters in the Gospels that refer to reincarnation. For example, Matthew; chapters, 11, 14, 16 and 17. Apparently, the early Church did not have a problem with the concept until 533 when the Second Council of Church Fathers deleted many direct references to reincarnation from the Bible, for their own reasons.

But I felt in conflict. Was I allowed to believe what seemed to make sense, but conflicted with what I had been taught? I needed to know more. I wanted to believe what I felt was true.

I thought of the advice our Pastor, Father Gavigan had given me long ago: "Read Edgar Cayce." I had, and it was the beginning of my acceptance of the reality of a life before this one.

By now I was beginning to feel quite comfortable with the fact that this was not my first time on the planet. But why don't we remember our past lives? I would find some time later, there is a very good reason why. *Another book.*

But 'previous lives' would have a great impact on my under-standing the happenings in my life in the following years.

CHAPTER 8

With the doctor and the lawyer now out of the picture, all I had to go on were the date and time of birth, and the name of the hospital. I contacted the hospital in Philadelphia, which was still in operation, and requested a copy of my records for that period of time.

"Those records have been archived and are no longer available," I was told. "I am very sorry, but they have most likely been destroyed by now. That was twenty years ago."

No matter whom I asked it was like a broken record. No one knew anything and all information was somewhere in the ether. Later I would learn that all OB records must be kept for twenty-one years, but I did not know enough then to question the woman any further.

I found myself in the depths of discouragement. But

something inside me kept repeating, "Do not give up." I felt I had to let it go for the moment, trusting that God heard my plea and He would point me in the right direction, or lead me to someone who would, at the right time.

In the meantime, life at home was becoming more unpleasant every day. I realized that anything I did to attempt to find my daughter had to be kept from my husband. "If I ever find out you are looking for that kid of yours, I will throw you out of this house along with all your belongings—and I'll tell everyone why." In his mind I was nothing but "damaged goods," and I believed he would indeed shame me among everyone who knew us. Such was my mindset, thanks to my rigid upbringing.

By this time, however, the drive to find my daughter was intense. I decided I had to disarm Charles... take away his ammunition. I would reveal my "awful" secret myself.

I carefully selected the woman I would tell about the baby and the adoption. She was in our home daily, and while I did not ask her to keep my secret, she said she would not tell anyone. Even so, I knew it was only a matter of time before my secret would be out.

Still, Charles continued to hold my "shameful past" over my head. He continually threatened to throw me out and I believed he would do it. What's more, I could not afford to challenge him. I had five children at home, and they were still in school. My greatest fear was that he would refuse to pay the older kids' college tuition if I crossed him. He had threatened to do this before, and I believed he would make good on his threat.

And so, I continued on with the plan to find my daughter. But now every move toward my goal had to be carefully thought out and enacted with the utmost caution.

Determination was one thing. But with all the normal channels blocked I had no idea where to turn next.

Shortly after my disappointing summer, however, little and important steps began to appear in strangely serendipitous ways.

In the grocery store one day, while waiting in a slow line, I noticed a small book sticking out of a revolving rack. It was titled, *The Adult Adoptee*. Carefully, I removed a copy and tucked it under the bread on the conveyer belt so no one would see me buying it. Once home, I hid it until I was alone and had time to read it.

Not long after, on a Sunday afternoon, I was leafing through the Sunday supplement section of the newspaper—and there was an article about the Adoption Forum of Philadelphia. It was a recently formed group of adult adoptees searching for their birthparents. My heart almost stopped beating. What if my daughter was there, looking for *me?* I couldn't wait to contact them or attend the meetings myself.

Again: Charles. I knew I could not call from the

house, because it would show up on our phone bill. So I asked my friend—the woman I had told about the adoption—and she readily agreed to let me use her phone. There were no cell phones in the Seventies.

The Forum, I learned, met once a month and while they were essentially adoptees, they welcomed me with open arms. Now I had to find a reason to get up to Philadelphia. My younger brother who was divorced and lived alone, always welcomed my visits, and he lived not far from where the Forum met. Hastily, I planned a week-end visit to Tommy. Though only in his forties, he had suffered a heart attack a few years prior and it seemed logical for me to be checking on him. Even as possessive, suspicious, and controlling as he was, Charles would not question that.

My first contact with this wonderful group of people opened my eyes to something about which I was totally unaware. It had never occurred to me that my daughter might have issues that derived from being adopted. All the adopted kids I'd known while growing up were happy, well adjusted, even a little spoiled. I had imagined all these years, that she would be like that, too. But I learned that quite the opposite could be true. The adult men and women in this group not only had an instinctive desire to know who their birthparents were, they all felt that some part of them was missing. On one hand, as a birth mother, I was glad to find that I was not alone in these feelings; on the other hand it saddened me greatly to think that my daughter might have similar feelings. *Now, I really had to find her and dispel any thoughts she might have of being "given away."*

I formed a ready bond with this group and began to travel to Philadelphia as often as possible to attend meetings. The members of the Forum were professionals, housewives, secretaries, CEOs and simple working people. We all had a common bond, and I started to experience support and understanding in my quest for the truth.

I was learning so much about the "Adoption Triangle," the birthmother, the adoptee and the adoptive parents— and the effect that adoption had on all three. It almost consumed me. Between my brother and my friend, Claire, I had good coverage when I went to Philadelphia but I was afraid of arousing Charles' suspicions so I backed off after a couple of these monthly visits.

Still, I wanted to stay in touch with the Adoption Forum, especially now that I would not be attending the meetings for a while. To do this, I rented a P.O. Box in the next town where I could receive information from them. Every week someone would write me, and once a month, the newsletter came, and always, with it, *encouragement*. I finally had someone to talk to about adoption, my feelings, and how to initiate a search.

Stealth was still the name of the game. And I told my

new friends from Philadelphia that it was OK to call me, and I let them know times when Charles would not be at home. I could not call any of them, however, because I still could not have a call to show up on our phone bill. Even with the stress of having to be secretive, I found a surge of energy in the hope that now surrounded me. Hope that I was being pointed in the right direction.

During one of the meetings, the group suggested that I contact the birth father. "Very often they know something you don't. Maybe your OB let something slip. You said they were colleagues. Try to look him up. It's worth a try."

I had no idea where he was, or how to find him, but I remember Claire telling me she heard he had moved to New England shortly after I left Philadelphia.

A day or two after our conversation I was driving past the County Medical Society building, when something inside me just *clicked*. I had this crazy idea to go inside and ask the secretary, who I knew socially, if it was possible to locate a physician's address if I only had a name.

"Of course," she said. "Here, let me help you look."

"No, that's quite all right," I said, "I'd rather look myself."

She handed me the *National Register of Physicians*, which listed every physician in the country, showing all current information, including address and phone number.

And sure enough, there was his contact information.

The initial thought of contacting him was frightening. I was not sure if I could even handle hearing his voice. Not certain of his marital status, and afraid he might not want to talk to me I waited for several days before calling him. I also had to make certain my husband would not be home.

Fortunately, Charles was playing in a golf tournament that week, and I placed the call when I knew he was just starting his 'round. This time, I wanted to talk from my own home and my friend allowed me to charge the call to her number. I would pay her for the long-distance calls.

He answered the phone himself. I recognized his familiar voice—the quiet, firm way he had of speaking— and I fortified myself against remembering anything more. He said he was happy to hear from me and told me he never did get divorced.

I did not hesitate, nor did I chit-chat. I got right to the point. "Steve, I want to find our daughter, and wonder if you have any idea who adopted her. I know you and Dr. S. talked. Anything he might have told you would help me."

He was quiet for a minute, as though absorbing what I had just said.

"Please don't do this Nancy," he said, firmly. "Please leave well enough alone. You don't want to upset her life. She's probably very happy... and she may not even know she's adopted."

My thoughts raced back to the adult adoptees I had recently met. "I can't, I said. "She has a right to know why she was adopted and I have a right to know who my child is."

Again, a thoughtful silence. He never was one to just blurt something out, and always took his time before speaking.

Then, he gave me a more secure phone number on which to reach him and asked me to call him in a few days. "In the meantime, please think of all the ramifications if you do decide to keep looking."

When I hung up I knew there was no need to entertain his idea for a minute. I had already thought of the ramifications of my searching, as well as the possibility she may not know she was adopted. I would deal with those issues at a later time.

I waited a few days before calling him back. This time he seemed a bit more understanding. "You really do want to find her, don't you?" he said.

"Yes I really do."

"It's *that* important to you?"

"It is that important."

"I can't help you from up here, and I have absolutely no information. But I do know someone who would probably be able to help, and he'd do anything for you."

Then he asked if I remembered his German friend, Walter. I remembered this man only too well. He often came along when Steve would drop by to say hello, and he'd walk several paces behind us when Steve and I would be strolling down the street or on a path around the grounds. He was quiet, and did not say much even when he spoke, probably because his English was not good back then, but he was always well dressed, and drove an expensive car.

One day I asked Steve about their close connection, because the only thing they seemed to have in common was that they both spoke German. He told me he operated on Walter's hand once in an emergency situation and they had just stayed friends.

"Well, he makes me nervous, I wish you would not bring him around so often," I'd said. Steve had laughed. "He's harmless… and he just thinks you're pretty."

"Is that why he stares at me?" I'd responded, flustered. "Well, it makes me uncomfortable."

There was something else about him that made me uneasy, even from the start, but I could not put my finger on it.

Now, here I was with Walter crossing the path of my life again. Why now?

"Yes, I remember him," I said. "But how can he help?"

Steve told me that Walter had started his own electrical contracting business and had done very well. He built a luxury home in the area, but then got divorced, the house was sold and he wasn't sure where he was now living. "The point is, he has plenty of contacts and knows influential people all over the place. Walter was always very fond of you, and every time we got together over the years, he would ask if I had heard from you or if I knew where you were."

"I'll give you his office address and you can contact him there. I'm sure he'll be more than happy to help you."

Again, the strange uneasiness. I was not sure I wanted to contact Walter, but thanked Steve anyway. He asked me to keep in touch and let him know if I found out anything.

When I hung up, however, I was fairly certain this was the last contact we would have. Since Steve was not able to help me, I saw no reason to keep in touch. The scene I anticipated if Charles found I was searching for my daughter was bad enough. I could only imagine the scene if he found out I had been in touch with her father.

And now I sensed something was about to happen, though I was not sure what. The last thing I needed was more opposition—not from Charles or anyone. Nor did I need complications—like contact with Walter. The subtle feeling that I was now, finally, on the right track began to grow.

CHAPTER 9

I ALLOWED a few weeks to lapse, then decided to "go visit my friend, Claire" in Philadelphia.

The Adoption Forum members were glad to see me, but I was much happier to see them that Sunday. I found that a few more birth mothers had now joined the group. Working together lightened the load as we helped one another.

We shared with each other any information we were fortunate to discover, for even the simplest item might turn up to be important.

If someone got a name, we all jumped in. We kept abreast of legislation, and new laws that were evolving as searches were beginning to break the old mold of silence, and heartbreak. The current laws were unnatural and stood in opposition to a mother's basic right to know. It also violated an adult adoptee's right to know their own history and background.

Though on opposite sides of the adoption triangle, we were all searching for the same thing... *a name.*

Without a name, there was no possibility of finding our biological part. If an agency was involved, there would at least be records, and though sealed, there may be ways, albeit difficult and expensive, but they could be unsealed. In some parts of the country registries had been set up but only valuable if both adoptee and birthmother had agreed to be contacted and were on the same registry. A minimally effective method back then.

In a private adoption there is no agency. Information is known only to the birthparent, the adoptive parents, the physician and the attorney. With the physician and attorney out of the picture, I was on my own.

I desperately needed a copy of the *amended* birth certificate which would give me her name. Obtaining a copy of that sealed document was next to impossible without a court order.

As we observed the methods the adoptees were using to gain a copy of their *original birth certificate* — —we realized that the same method they used might work for us, as well.

Even an *animal* has the instinct to search for a lost offspring, and goes about it with a vengeance until it is found. That is pretty much how I saw this group. A mother wants to know what became of her child. And beyond that, we believed we had a *right*.

We attempted to work within the confines of the law, but it was futile. We found our adoption laws to be archaic and the courts unrelenting.

Many of us set out to change those laws. We spoke to legislators, wrote letters to Congress, addressed groups representing various sides of the Adoption Triangle, and got the attention of the media. But those changes would take time and we were running out of time. Birthparents were ageing, our children were marrying and moving from the area where they were adopted. We could not wait for the changes.

All we could do in the meantime was to persevere and use whatever means we could to connect with our past. We braved the establishment, and were forced to circumvent the unfair laws.

I attempted to obtain the birth certificate several times without any luck. So I let it rest for a while and then approached the agency a third time.

On August 1, 1980, on my daughter's twenty-fourth birthday, I received a letter in the mail from the Bureau of Vital Statistics. Inside, I stared with disbelief, as I tearfully read the name of my child and her adoptive parents. Charlene_____.

Was I being invasive? She had been an adult for three

years now, and I had kept my promise not to interfere in her life to this point.

I no longer had any reservations about looking for her.

My joy was indescribable. The first thing I did was to thank God. *Now that I knew her name, surely, He wouldn't let me get this far and not find her.*

When I made the decision to begin searching for my daughter, I first discussed it with the other children who were then sixteen, fifteen, thirteen and seven. The baby was only months old. They were by my side the whole time and would frequently ask me "if anything came in the mail today?"

I couldn't wait to give them this news. When I did, it seemed to make her more real to them, and to me, especially.

The next day I called a member of the Adoption Forum, also a birthmother. At the last meeting she gave me her phone number and said I could call her anytime. Her husband was cooperating in her search, which only emphasized the hurt I felt over Charles' hateful attitude. When I called to tell her my good news, she began to cry...tears of joy for someone else... such was the bond we had with one another.

The next day, while Charles was playing golf, I called Steve—her father.

When I told him what her name was, his only comment was, "*We* should have named her!"

What stood out to me, though, was her middle name. *Louise*.

My mother-in-law's name was *Louise*. Charles' daughter from his first marriage was Charlotte *Louise*, and *our* oldest daughter was Cara *Louise*.

Was it possible these four women were connected by more than a name?

An interesting thought, but I cast that thought aside and moved on.

The following week, I managed to get back up to Philadelphia and the Adoption Forum. I shared her name with them, hoping someone might recognize it. Their advice was to look in all the local phone directories and see if it was in there. I could not stay in Philadelphia.

I found out it was possible to get copies of out of state phone directories mailed to me. I ordered a copy of the white pages from every surrounding county of Philadelphia and they were soon delivered to my P.O. box in Virginia. When they arrived, I looked through every one and I did not leave until I had searched through every one, at least two times. I found no listing in any of them under that last name.

Discouraged, I tossed the books in the trash and went home more discouraged than ever. Maybe the doctor was right, they *were* from out of state, or maybe they moved away shortly after her birth. *Then how did I account for sensing her presence and just knowing she was in the Philadelphia area and at the Jersey shore all those summers?*

I had no choice but to accept the fact that they did not live in the area.

When it became obvious this might be the case, I decided to put my own search on hold and help others. I found that I was more effective without my own emotions involved and was able to connect several adoptees with their birthmothers that first year. It had been over a year since I had scoured the phone books and while I accepted the fact that I needed a different kind of help, I continued to help others.

In the meantime, my life at home had become a war zone. My husband's behavior had deteriorated into total hatred. I could not talk to him, much less rationalize with him, and it appeared his alcohol use was now being fortified with drugs. His abusive words had escalated into abusive behavior. Since I was not talking about my search, and I believed he had no idea I was involved in it, something else was going on within him.

The following Halloween a violent incident occurred at home which forced me to leave my home that night.

When Steve learned I had not yet contacted Walter he gave him my home phone number. I had not wanted Steve to know how unstable my marriage was, so never mentioned it to him during our phone calls. He had no idea that his attempt to help me would result in a disaster.

This event and what led up to it was described in an

earlier book.

Charles had hit me, knocking me to the floor.

After cleaning the blood from my face and calming my nine -year- old son who witnessed the incident, I called a good friend who was an attorney. He advised me to leave the house, spend the night at a friends', or a hotel, and not go home until Charles moved out. In addition, he said to me, "Nancy, this time, you must file charges, if you don't, he will kill you one of these days." His behavior had become that violent. I respected this attorney friend and took his advice.

I spent the night at a friend's home, and the next morning I left, taking the three younger children with me, and headed up to Philadelphia where my brother lived. I expected to stay no more than two weeks. I would end up staying three years.

But before I left Virginia, I went to the Magistrate's office and filed charges of physical abuse.

Those three years were fraught with emotion, fear, threats, harassment, and yet, an unbelievable peace...I was out of his house, away from him and in my own space. But even more rewarding, I could now openly continue the search for my daughter, and I was near those who could help me the most. In the meantime, I would continue to help others. It gave my life purpose and eased the sadness that I might not find my own child.

In one instance, I worked very hard to find the adopted

son of a good friend of mine, Jeannine, another birth-mother. He was born on New Year's Eve and I wanted so much to find him by that time that year. I spent the entire Christmas time doing research and making phone calls.

On December 31st, I got the information I had been looking for: his name, address and phone number. When I called Jeannine, who by now had moved out of the area, she and I both were crying. Again, tears of joy.

If you never gave up a child, you can't imagine how overwhelming this feels.

CHAPTER 10

IN SOME WAYS, light *was* dawning into my life.

I experienced unusual moments when I *knew* I was on the right path however chaotic my life was thanks to the nightmarish marriage and the struggle to find my daughter...It was that inner, gut feeling that I was doing what I *had* to do. And at other moments the spiritual experiences seemed like a fantasy...or at least they didn't seem to impact my need for everyday, real help. Just figuring out the right move to make was burdensome. If only I could count on help from *somewhere.*

Within a few weeks of our move to Philadelphia, my close friend, Father Murphy drove up to check out the house where the children and I were staying. He saw we were comfortable and safe, but suggested I find a place of my own if I was going to be staying in the area. At that point, I expected to be back in my own home in Virginia within weeks. I let him know these arrangements were temporary and the place would be fine for now.

When it became obvious that Charles was not moving out, I realized I could not legally keep a nine year old out of school for any length of time, so enrolled Jon in the local parochial school. That meant I would need to stay put until the end of the school year, which was eight months away. *How would I manage? Our needs felt overwhelming.*

First of all, during those months, I lived like a fugitive on the run. Because of Charles' threats to have someone kidnap the children, Jenny and Jon were never out of my sight, and I was aware of every vehicle that might be following me.

One morning I found footprints in the snow outside one of the bedroom windows in Walter's house where we were now living. I called Walter who came over immediately. He called the police, who determined that one of the two sets of prints appeared to belong to a woman. The other set, to a large man. In addition, car keys had been dropped as though they left in a hurry.

I recalled that the night before, I'd heard strange sounds from outside and thought it was the wind or a branch hitting the house. To be safe, I'd turned on all the outside lights.

"That must have frightened them away," the officer said.

The stress was horrible.

If Charles' goal was to inflict mental and physical torment, he had succeeded. In addition, I had the total responsibility for my elderly cousin, Sara, and frequently needed to go to Reading, which was one hour away. Jon was in school, but I still had Jenny at home and it was difficult to do what I needed to with a three year old along.

I wasn't ready yet, to ask Walter to watch her while I went to Reading.

In an attempt to help myself in some way, I began to drive around to familiarize myself with the area, and at least get a feel where I might want to live, should I decide to move later. But was this the right place for me? How would I know? If only I had a clear sign.

One day, I ventured in a different direction from the area we were now living and ended up in Villanova, a suburb of Philadelphia. While admiring the lovely old homes along the road, I spotted a beautiful mansion that sat back off the road, and I slowed down. The large sign on the property read; "Notre Dame de Namur." Could this be the Motherhouse of the nuns that taught me in DC? I spent four wonderful years at Notre Dame Academy in Washington, DC taught by these highly educated women.

I need to feel connected to something familiar, I thought.

I pulled into the driveway, unstrapped Jenny from her car seat and we walked up to the front door. I rang the doorbell, and a few minutes later a grey haired lady in a plain housedress opened the door, and when I explained myself, invited us in.

I told her why I stopped and she just looked at me and smiled. "You don't know who I am do you," she said.

"No, I'm afraid I don't," I replied, studying her.

"Well, I know who *you* are. You are Nancy Moore, and I taught you at K St."(which is how the nuns referred to Notre Dame Academy in Washington.) She was Sister Catherine Julie, my home- room teacher when I was a junior in high school. I did not recognize her in civilian dress as the nuns wore habits back then…

She led Jenny and me into a parlor off the massive entrance foyer. "Sit down, and tell me what's going on."

I brought her up to date leaving out some things not necessary for her to know.

As I spoke, Sr. Catherine Julie was beginning to look familiar, even in civilian clothes. She had a remarkable memory.

"I remember when you did not come back to school for two weeks after your uncle died," she recalled. "I thought they buried you with him." I vividly remembered my answer to her thirty- plus years before. "I wish they had," I had answered. I was so distraught over Uncle Jack's death.

Changing the subject, she looked over at Jenny and asked me how old she was.

"Three- and- a half."

"Well, she should be in our Montessori school next door."

When I pulled into the driveway, I noticed a long one story building out back with a sign that said, "Launfal," but with no idea what it was —though I *was* familiar with Montessori schools as my other four children had attended the one in McLean.

"In fact, we'll just go over there right now and I'll introduce you to the woman who runs the school and"... she was up and moving already..."I will see to it that there is a place for Jenny, and she can probably start this week."

After looking at the school, Jenny seemed excited. She wanted to go to school just like her big brother, Jon.

It suddenly dawned on me that this meant my three year old would be in school, freeing me up to care for Sara, and in a place where I had ties. We signed a document that stated she could not be picked up by *anyone* but me.

I was elated. At least something was happening on a positive note. I thanked Sister Catherine Julie profusely and as we said good-bye, she took my hand and said, "I believe it was the Hand of God that led you here today."

I paused. I knew she was right. Not by accident, another critical issue in my life had been settled.

And little by little, the Hand of God and the hands of those He sent to help me, would continue to show me the way. And just maybe, help me find my daughter.

As the months went on, I decided to seriously look for another place to move when school was out. I knew it offended Walter after all he had done to make his house comfortable for us, but Charles saw it differently, and I needed to be on my own turf in order to deal with his erratic off- the- wall behavior.

I had repeatedly asked Charles to leave Walter out of this. " He wouldn't be in the picture *at all* if he had not seen you hit me." I told him. "And now with all your threats and the other things you are doing, he feels the need to protect us. "

I was wasting words. Charles was obsessed with the belief that "Walter stole my wife," and repeatedly made this statement. It was more than absurd, but his belief system was totally rooted in that lie.

But being in Walter's proximity seriously complicated things. On one hand, I did not want this man in my life. His presence was creating havoc. On the other hand, without him, I would have had no place to go—and with my life threatened, I had the protection I needed.

By this time I'd come to believe that people come into our lives when we need them, but it was many years later before I realized that Walter was in our lives for a most unusual purpose.

When school was out, I moved into the townhouse in Paoli that I had found by just driving around. Father Murphy again came up to check it out and was pleased with the place. It looked safe and comfortable. I did not mention to him my suspicions of being followed, and hoped that maybe it would stop when I moved into my own place.

Living in Philadelphia continued to be a contest of wits as I attempted to maintain a semblance of order and peace for the children and myself amidst the ongoing harassing by my husband and those he engaged to do his dirty work.

But living there did have its advantages. With Sara now in her nineties, and only an hour away, I was able to keep a better eye on her. Occasionally, I would bring her to stay with us for a week or so, and then take her back to her home where she lived by herself. But as her general health began to deteriorate, so did her mental status and I eventually found it necessary to move her into an assisted living facility.

On one of my visits to her, I pulled into the parking garage of her facility, and as I rounded a sharp curve, I heard something fall out from under the car. I stopped, looked under the car and found a round object I did not recognize. I picked it up, planning to stop by a garage on the way home to see what it was, but since the car was running OK, I forgot about it.

Later, I showed it to Walter.

His face was grim. "It's a tracking device." He walked over and threw it in the trash.

I felt violated and angry. "Did *you* put it on the car to see where I was going?"

"Of course not! I would never do that," he responded.

"Then who did?"

It was only too obvious in *my* thinking that when Charles and my son, Jeff, had been up over the previous week-end, Charles might have attached it to my car. There was snow on the ground and I would have noticed if any tracks led to my car, but did not recall seeing any, besides, there was not time for Charles to have done it. It remained a puzzle and I continued to obsess over it. Much later, I would find that it was part of a much larger problem, and was connected to the parties ordered to follow me.

Such were the things I dealt with on a continuing basis.

In the meantime, I kept busy trying to furnish the house I was renting. Forbidden to take any of my household items or furniture from the home in Virginia, I was forced to furnish this new place from scratch. With minimal resources, I frequented the used furniture stores and auctions when the children were in school.

Aside from furnishing the house, I enjoyed the extra time I was now spending with the more frequent Adoption

Forum meetings and the friends I had met there. Every moment with these people was valuable. You never knew when just one little word might lead to something helpful. By now I was comfortable leaving both children in Walter's care. He was very attached to them, they liked him and I knew they were safe.

Since the incident of finding footprints in the snow, Walter had become a very protective presence in our lives. I was still afraid Charles would carry out his threat to have someone steal the children, and I welcomed Walter's protection. While his presence in my life had a negative impact on my dealings with Charles, I felt much safer when he was nearby, but it was emotionally exhausting.

With little happening in my search, one of the members of the AF suggested I contact a well- known psychic in Philadelphia. She routinely read for the Mayor and other prominent figures, so I made an appointment with her.

This woman ran a tight ship and got right to the point. She did not ask why I was there, but rather, boldly told me what *she* felt I needed to know. It was a most interesting reading, connecting the people in my present life to the many past lives we lived together. Though I was astounded at her revelations, I was more interested in her help in finding my daughter.

Finally, she said to me, "I don't know why you are up *here* looking for her. She's closer to *your* home—she's near water."

"But will I *find* her?" I asked.

"Yes, you will find her. *It will all fall into place.*"

All fall into place? I left her large row house with a head full of information, not all of it related to my daughter's whereabouts. While the reading clarified much of my current issues, uppermost in my mind were these words:

Yes, you will find your daughter.

Now, I wanted to find Kathryn, my late Uncle's companion. She would want to know that I was looking for my child that was adopted. Kathryn was so much a part of my early life and was there for me when I was pregnant. I wanted her to know what was happening in my life now. I remember her saying to me when I was pregnant, "It is a crime that two people who love each other can not find a way to be together." And when she found out I was putting the baby up for adoption, she said that it was *unfair*. She was as upset as I was back then, and I needed her to be a comforting part of my life again.

I admired and loved Kate, as Uncle Jack called her. She understood me and often came to my defense when I was a child. If either of my parents acted in too harsh a manner where I was concerned, she spoke out. I once heard her say to them, after I had been given a string of orders, "Mary and Guy, for God's sake, she's only a child! Let her be a child, those things shouldn't be her responsibility." I remember my father's reply. "Well, she's the oldest and it *is* her responsibility."

Kathryn taught me more about 'girl things' than Mom did and I could talk to her more easily than I could to my mother. I felt very close to this stunningly beautiful woman.

For this reason, Kathryn was the family member I confided in when I was pregnant and she and her sister Anna faithfully visited me in Philadelphia during those awful months, years ago. But I did not have her new name or address. She married late in life and had sent me a letter telling me this when I was living in McLean. I had no idea where her letter was or who I could call to find out. My mother did not have her new address either, and wasn't sure of her last name. Without her name, I could not look her up. Even though most of my reading material those days had been phone books, none were very helpful in finding a name I hoped to recognize. It was frustrating. Yet, I *really* wanted her to know I was trying to find my daughter. She would be so happy.

With every step I made to find my daughter now, the path grew even steeper.

In order to appease Charles and his attorney, I agreed to his bi-monthly visits with the children. I preferred to drive down from Philadelphia to McLean rather than have him come up and invade my peaceful space. On one of those week-ends, shortly after I arrived at the house to pick up the children, I went into the kitchen to retrieve one of my sharp knives which I badly needed in Philadelphia. I had purchased them before we were married, and had every right to take one.

"Put that back," he ordered. "If you want something from this house, you move back. You are not to take *anything* out of this house!" I was angry at the injustice of what was happening, but I put the knife down and quickly walked out of the kitchen toward the den where the children were watching TV.

As I walked toward the den, I stopped to pick up a piece of paper lying beside a very narrow bookcase where I had kept some paperbacks. As I reached down to pick it up I recognized the familiar handwriting. *My heart almost stopped.* It was the letter Kathryn had sent me years ago with her new name and address on it. I had tucked it in between the paperbacks years ago and had forgotten where I put it.

How did this piece of paper get on the floor? And right at this moment, too?

It couldn't have been there all along. It must have fallen out just as I was walking past it. There were lots of other little papers I had tucked in between the books, why had *this one* fallen out?

All I could think of on the way back to Paoli was calling her as soon as we got home.

The drive back to Pennsylvania seemed to take forever.

As soon as I arrived at our townhouse, I got the children settled and dialed Kathryn's number. Her husband answered the phone. I identified myself as an old family friend, and said I would like to talk to Kathryn, it was important.

"Well, you'd better hurry," he said. "She's in St. Joseph's Hospital, dying of leukemia. You can visit her if you want, but she won't know you—hasn't recognized me for more than a week. So I don't go bother going over that often."

My heart sank. I called Walter and asked him to hurry over and please watch the children, I had to go to Reading.

At the Nurses Station on Kathryn's floor, the nurse gave me her room number but warned me she was totally unresponsive...had been that way for over a week. "She doesn't even recognize the nurse who takes care of her every day, and it's the woman who lived next door to her for years."

The door to Kathryn's room was ajar, and I walked in. She was lying there so still and peaceful. I stood for a moment and watched her breathing... her chest slowly rising and falling with each breath. No groaning, or gasping, just in and out, quiet breathing. Kathryn was simply lying there, with her arms gently resting on top of the smooth bedspread. Her beautiful black hair, now a silver gray. The afternoon sun cast a lovely glow across the room as it shone below the partially drawn shade. No IV in her arm, no oxygen tube in her nose. But what impressed me the most was the absence of all the usual paraphernalia usually found in a hospital room.

I thought to myself, *This is the way I want to die. Peacefully, in a clean, uncluttered room, beneath smooth sheets. No tubes, IV's or stuff all over the place.*

The vision before me was pure Kathryn.

I tried to hold back the tears... Now, she would never know. Wouldn't even know I had been here for that matter....

Then, I saw her move slightly, as though to ease a stiff body part.

I moved in close to her bed and leaned down to whisper in her ear. "Kathryn, I realize you probably can't hear me, but it's Nancy. I came as soon as I found out you were here. I am so sorry I haven't been in touch, but I couldn't find your new last name and phone number until today." Even if she was unable to respond, I wanted her to know I was there and had not forgotten her.

To my amazement, she stirred again—then opened her eyes and turned her head toward me.

"It's good you have come, Nance. I can't believe he let you get away. Does he know you are here?"

For a second I wondered if she knew who she was talking to, but she'd called me Nance, not Nancy. She always called me Nance.

"I left him, Kathryn, I moved out a year ago and am living in Philadelphia with the two younger children. And I am looking for the baby I had that was adopted."

"I am glad you left him," she said. "And I hope you find her." Her voice was soft, not labored, and had her familiar ring to it. She seemed lucid, but I did not want to tire her any further. I just wanted to sit beside her for a while, and then I would leave. So I pulled a chair up beside her bed and took her hand.

But she wanted to talk. She told me about her illness, the unsuccessful therapy, and her request to avoid any extreme life saving measures. "I just want to die in peace," she said. She pointed to her wrinkled, dry arms and asked how I liked her *beautiful* skin.. Her sense of humor was still intact. Kathryn always had the most beautiful, tan skin.

Then, "I need to tell you something," she said. Her voice, still clear, but soft. And she was awake, not in a coma. "I am sorry I said those things about you, but I was sick at the time but when we don't feel well, we say things we don't mean."

I had no idea what she was talking about but she was very sure of what she was saying.

"Don't worry," I said, only wanting to put her at ease. "Just forget it."

"It's bothered me and I needed to tell you I was sorry."

"Kathryn, you never hurt me," I said, "Please remember that."

She breathed in a deep sigh, then turned her head toward me again. "Where's My Boy?" she asked. My eyes filled up because that is what she always called Uncle Jack.

"Kathryn, Jack died a long time ago…," but she did not let me finish.

I saw her smile, and noticed she was looking beyond the foot of the bed—over to the side of the room. Her voice became much clearer, and she raised her head slightly and began talking, but not to me.

"There he is, there's My Boy!" she said with a happy look on her face. "Don't you see him, Nance?" she said, pointing in the direction she was looking.

I looked, but of course, did not see him.

But in that moment…on this late hot summer afternoon…I felt a sudden rush of cold air brush past me. This was not a puff of air as an air-conditioner might put out. I sensed a *presence*. It was so very strong!

Chills ran up and down my spine, as tears freely ran down my face, and I stifled a sob. Uncle Jack *was* there. I was certain of it.

I was still shaking as I saw her lay her head back down on the pillow. That beautiful look still on her face… she reached for my hand. "Promise to come back again, Nance," she whispered.

"Of course, I will," I reassured her.

She closed her eyes and I kissed her good-bye.

When I left I was engulfed in a sense of awe, and peace at what I had just experienced.

As I walked past the nurses' station on my way out,

one of the nurses stopped me. "That's your mother, isn't it? " she said, as though she believed it was.

I was too teary to answer so just nodded my head affirmative. She *had* been like a mother to me. "I thought so," she answered.

"You were in there over an hour, just sitting beside your dying mother and she was not even aware you were there. How beautiful."

How could I tell her? I was too caught up in the moment, even if I wanted to tell her how wrong she was.

And yes, it was more than beautiful. My beloved Uncle Jack had visited us both, but would only be taking Kathryn back.

I found the one -hour drive home to Paoli a quiet time of reflection for me. So many difficult things were happening in my life, that I often felt abandoned. But today brought a new sense of upliftment and reassurance to me. I was not forgotten.

Someone had put that paper where I would see it. Kathryn did not want to die without asking forgiveness for something hurtful she had once said about me. It did not matter to me, but it seemed to bother her. And I had evidence that Uncle Jack was alive somewhere, and had come to not only comfort the woman he had loved in this life, but to take her home.

Kathryn died a couple days later... peacefully... just as she wished.

And not only had I had been able to tell her that I was looking for my child, I'd had more evidence that forces from beyond do indeed come to our assistance.

I would need that knowledge soon.

CHAPTER 11
(PAOLI, PENNSYLVANIA - 1981)

IN THE WEEKS that followed, I felt a terrible sadness over Kathryn's death, but at the same time, I felt even more closely connected to the spirit world. On more than one occasion I have been present when a person very close to death, begins "talking" to someone we cannot see. Often these conversations are accompanied by a wonderful sense of peace. I believe that when a soul is ready to leave the earth plane and close to the "other side," they are able to communicate with those family members already there. I find this comforting.

I never told anyone of Uncle Jack's visit there in Kathryn's room, afraid it would have been met with too much skepticism. Instead, I kept busy caring for Sara and dealing with her minor crises, keeping tabs on the

children's progress at school, and trying to avoid Charles'
continuous and harassing phone calls.

The Adoption Forum had now begun trying to change
the adoption laws, and I jumped on-board with my offer
to help. They continued to be an uplifting force in my
life and I kept hoping for that one lead I so desperately
needed.

If I could not find my daughter, I could at least help to
change the laws so others could. I intuitively felt I would
be guided to the right people at the right time, so did not
obsess over it.

One morning, while reading the Philadelphia *Inquirer*,
I turned to a column written by Darrell Sifford. In it
he quoted from a recently published book, *The Psychotic
Personality*, written by Drs. Leon Saul and Silas Warner.
I was taken aback by how closely it mimicked my husband's behavior. I needed to talk to Dr. Saul...and as
soon as possible.

I couldn't believe how easy it was to contact the man.
I found his name in the phone book and called him. I told
him briefly why I wanted to meet him and he suggested I
come to his home in Media. "It's rather close to Paoli," he
said. At his suggestion, I went over that afternoon. It was
a warm summer day and we sat out in his garden, where
we could, as he put it, "talk among the birds and nature."

I found myself in the company of a delightful gentleman in his eighties, slightly built but a giant in his

field. He was now Professor Emeritus of Psychiatry at University of Pennsylvania Medical School, where he had been on the faculty since 1948.

I was honored that he would take his valuable time to speak to a stranger. I could be a nut case for all he knew.

For the next two hours, we discussed my marriage, the separation and my present situation. Dr. Saul then excused himself for a few minutes and went up into the house. "I'll be right back, don't go away," he said, smiling.

A few moments later I watched with awe and respect, as this delightful man walked across the lawn and sat down on the bench opposite me. Shortly, his lovely wife appeared, carrying two glasses of iced tea. "Are you sure you're not too warm out here?" she asked. "No, it's fine and I'll be leaving soon." I thanked her for the tea. "Take your time," she said.

As I watched his elderly wife walk back to the house, a sudden, but painful reality jolted me: *I will never know the comfort of growing old with someone I love, like these two.*

I assumed Leon Saul to be Jewish, but he said, "No, I am a Quaker, and have spent my life trying to keep couples together, but"...and he slid up to the edge of his bench and looked right at me. "...I am telling *you* to leave your husband as soon as you can. Otherwise, he will destroy you. You must leave him."

"In the meantime I want you to make an appointment to see my partner, Silas Warner. I am about to retire and he is a much younger man. While you don't need a psychiatrist, you do need someone to keep you in balance and preserve your sanity, given all the abnormality that is around you...and Silas would be good for you."

I felt that I had just spent an afternoon with God. *I was not crazy after all.*

For the next year and a half, I would meet with Dr. Warner at his home-office on a regular basis. These meetings enabled me to be more objective and I was better able to handle the frustrations I faced on a daily basis, to say nothing of validating my sanity.

When I was back home in Virginia, Charles would say to me, "You are sick and ought to be hospitalized." And then after I moved to Philadelphia, he would repeatedly tell me, "Someone is trying to make you think you are crazy." Over and over and over, I would hear this, and just as many times I would have to tell myself, *I am not crazy I am just over-stressed.* When I mentioned this to Dr. Warner during a session, he did not respond at first, but later, said, "You are being *gaslighted*, Nancy. Do you know what that means?" I did: It means that someone is trying to make you *think* you are crazy. The word comes from the title of the movie, *Gaslight*, in which a husband is trying to make his wife believe she is insane. The term is sometimes used in psychiatry to illustrate similar behavior.

My suspicion of being followed, and then, that

someone was trying to make me crazy *were* real. Afraid of sounding paranoid I'd kept those suspicions to myself.

But the fact was, someone *was* trying to upset my mental balance by giving me conflicting messages on a regular basis. That persons or persons, was intentionally lying to me, but who... Charles? Walter? The woman who was leaving messages on my phone?—and why?

I no longer knew who or what to believe, and *that* can make you crazy. I looked to Dr. Warner for direction and the reassurance, which he gave me.

Still, I felt that I wanted more clarification.

One day, while mulling things over, I thought of Anne Gehman, the medium who taught the classes I attended on metaphysics several years ago. I was so impressed with her back then, that I decided to look her up and make an appointment... She could see me the following week. I drove down to Virginia and back the same day, telling no one where I was going. Even if Anne extended her usual one-hour reading I could still be home by late-afternoon.

By now I felt comfortable leaving the children with Walter. He would kill anyone who attempted to harm or touch them. So I asked him to stay with the kids after school and until I got back. He enjoyed being with them and they were happy when he was around. I also knew he would have supper ready when I got home.

Anne was better known as a Medium, but was an equally gifted psychic. I was confident she could shed some light on my daughter's whereabouts, and help clarify the conflicting information I was receiving. My daughter was now twenty-three, and given the terrible opposition I was facing in my life, I was anxious to see Anne again and was looking forward to the reading.

After we greeted each other, she and I sat for a few moments of silence and centering. When Anne was ready, she began speaking. I had not told her why I wanted a reading, relying simply on the messages she would bring me. I waited.

"There is a man around you, and this has to do with him," she started out. "I see a woman with flour all over her hands and on her apron. She is in a kitchen and is speaking another language. She seems to be the cook in a large home during the war, because I see military uniforms around. It is Germany, I think. Her name is Maria, and she wants you to tell the man who is around you that she thinks of him often and continues to watch over him. Tell him she wishes she could give him extra goodies now and is glad to see how good a cook he has become. She wants him to know that she is around him often. It looks like a happy relationship. Do you understand any of this?" she said to me.

I did. But how could she have known a man of German descent had become an important part of my life just now?

She continued to read, and I was hoping each word

would be what I had come to hear.

"I now see a young woman with long hair...somewhere in this country. She is doing something with her hands, like this," and Anne put her hands together, as though molding an object. "She wants me to tell you not to let *anyone* sculpt your life for you. You must sculpt it for yourself. Others are trying to tell you what to do. Do not listen to them. You know what you must do. She tells me her name is Gloria. Does that ring a bell? "

I nodded, shocked at what she was telling me.

Then Anne put both hands around her neck suddenly, and said, "Oh!—there is a terrible pain in my neck. Something dreadful is happening!"

I wanted Anne to stop the reading, because I was afraid of what she might feel next, but did not want to disrupt her thought pattern. "Oh, that was awful," she said, still holding her neck. "I wonder what that was all about."

I explained that Gloria had been Walter's girlfriend years ago, when he first came to this country and before I knew him. She was a sculptress and sold many of her items at a fine price. She went to France on vacation one month and was killed in a horrible train wreck in which she was decapitated.

Slowly Anne lowered her hands onto her lap... "It's better now. It's going away, yes, I do feel better....Let's get back to the reading. You're away from your home, aren't you?"

I nodded affirmative, with a lump in my throat. "Well, I don't see you coming back right away…maybe another year or two."

Not what I wanted to hear. I was hoping Charles would move out when he saw I was not budging—but *two more years?*

Her face became grave. "Your husband is trying to destroy you. You have humiliated him by leaving and he wants to destroy your good name. It is also about money."

Another difficult thought for me to digest.

Anne gave me a few more messages and the reading was over. I was a bit disappointed that no mention of my search had come up and was mystified that she was given messages for Walter and not me. But I let it go. I thanked Anne, we gave each other a hug and I left.

Once in the car, I was on auto-pilot. Having driven this route so many times this past year, I could now concentrate on the reading without worrying about what road to take.

Then in a flash, I recognized that Anne had told me *exactly* what I needed to know.

I often wondered if Walter was making up those tales of his—endless stories of his life in Germany, especially his early life under Hitler and then during the war. If that was the case, he might also be making up what he was telling me about issues concerning Charles. I needed to know!

But when Anne mentioned Maria's message for Walter, I knew he had been honest about his life. Walter had often spoken about Maria. He told me that she had been hired as a young woman to help in his family's kitchen, back in Koblenz, Germany, and had eventually become the family cook. The children were forbidden in the kitchen, but as a child, Walter often would sneak in and Maria would give him extra goodies. He said that she was like a mother to him, and when he would come home from Oronianburg, the special school where six-year-olds were forced to go under Hitler's regime, he would run first to Maria who would hug him and give him a special treat. She loved him as her own child. They had a wonderful relationship and then he went off to war some years later.

Indirectly, Anne had told me who was telling me the truth and who was probably lying. While I did not want to believe it was Charles, I now recognized that he had the most to gain by deceiving me. I began to rethink things and came to the conclusion that it was *Charles,* not *Walter,* who was deliberately lying to me about important issues.

And I couldn't wait to tell Walter about Maria…

I was grateful to Anne for clarifying the confusion that was about to drive me crazy, and I could forgive her for not mentioning my daughter.

Perhaps she already knew that would be taken care of.

My mother came up with the children for the Holidays. I felt badly that the children and I were out of our home now for the second Christmas, and when I mentioned this to the older kids they responded with the best Christmas present they could ever have given me.

"Mom, please don't feel bad about not being in our house in Virginia," they said. "To us, home is wherever *you* are."

The kids took Nana back to Virginia with them after Christmas and I knew she would be back up soon again. I continued my searches for others, and with good response. I felt happy for them and knew that my day would come.

And it did.

One day, I answered the phone mid- day to hear an unfamiliar voice, yet the woman seemed to know me. "Nancy, I'm so glad you are home, I did not want to leave *this* message on your machine," she said.

The woman was an adult adoptee I had met a couple times at one of our AF meetings, but we had not been close. She was a legal secretary whose boss had just asked her to look up a phone number. (This was in the Eighties—no computers, no Caller ID, just the local phone books.)

She said she looked not once, but twice, because next to the name she was looking for was a name she had stored in her head for almost a year. *It was my daughter's last name, along with her address and phone number.*

I nearly dropped the receiver! I thanked her over and over and over. I could not thank her enough. I asked. And I had been heard and guided. And now I received. I knocked and the door was opened.

All in an instant, in one phone call, I suddenly found myself on the last leg of a journey that had already taken me over four years.

While I now knew what I had to do, I wasn't quite sure *how* to go about it. But I felt confident that those who had guided me these four years would not abandon me now.

Such was my confidence in them.

CHAPTER 12

WHEN I SAW the address, the first thing I thought was that I had been right all along. It was *not* my imagination... *She did grow up in Philadelphia! I always knew she was here!* I had felt her presence when I returned to Philadelphia after she was born, and never doubted she was nearby. I felt validated. Her adoptive parents did not come from out of state, as I was led to believe, they probably lived here all their lives.

But now that I had an address, I realized I could not simply mail a letter to her.

What if she no longer lived at that address. She was now twenty-five and, perhaps, had already moved out of the family home. I was also concerned that the letter might be intercepted by someone who didn't want her to connect with her birth mother, in which case she'd never know I was trying to contact her. Or, I would be left with the other dreaded scenario: *She would decide not to respond.*

There were too many "if's" and so I called my friend, Ann, from the Adoption Forum to see if she had any suggestions. She had grown up in a nearby area and might be able to help. Was there a way I could find out anything about my daughter…was it possible to find out where she went to school, or church? I found the local Catholic Church, but could I gain access to any records? Probably not.

When I showed Ann my daughter's address, she knew which high school she probably attended. Ann then suggested we go over to the high school and look at the yearbooks. The librarian couldn't possibly remember all the students who had graduated, so Ann felt confident she would be allowed to view the yearbooks if she said she was trying to locate some names of her classmates.

I was both anxious and excited as we drove across town that afternoon… I also felt confident I would recognize the blonde, blue-eyed girl that would resemble my other two daughters.

I just needed to see her face.

As luck would have it, the one yearbook we needed was missing. Ann spoke to the librarian who had 'no idea why it would be missing.' "No one is allowed to remove them from the library," she told us. It was just *missing.* So we attempted to see if her name was in a yearbook the previous or following years. Negative.

Totally discouraged, we left.

Not one to give up easily, Ann called the school a few days later and again, spoke to the librarian. The 'lost' book had found its way back onto the shelf, and so we returned that same day.

When Ann handed the heavy book to me I almost *ran* to the reading room. My heart was pounding.

I turned the pages carefully, until I reached the L's.

And there she was.

Seeing my child's picture for the first time filled me with both sadness and joy. Sadness that I had missed all those years of her growing up and joy to see what she really looked like. My eyes filled up and I was over-whelmed by the emotions I felt.

I did not need to look at the name beneath the photo to know this was my daughter, because I was suddenly confronted with a reality that had eluded me all these years...instead of a blonde, blue- eyed girl, I was looking at the face of a young girl with a full head of dark curly hair and brown eyes, and a very familiar smile. She was a carbon copy of ... not me, but her *father.*

And then, as I continued to look at her picture, some-thing else jolted me into another reality, and I began to shake ...not out of fear, but from the realization that I *had* seen her many times before...but had not recognized who she was.

This was the face in my recurring dreams...the adult in a line of babies that I did not recognize as belonging to me because of her dark, curly hair.

"I see a young woman around you with a full head of dark, curly hair and brown eyes," I had once been told by a psychic. To whom I replied, "I am not sure who you are talking about."

I was overjoyed at finally seeing what she looked like, but totally unprepared for how much she resembled her father. She was truly beautiful.

Ann handed me a tissue, and then she wiped her own eyes. I was trembling with emotion and I could not thank this friend enough. As I put my arms around her shoulders I reassured her I'd be her birthmother until we found *her own* birthmother.

On the way home I told Ann that I wanted to see the house where my daughter lived. Maybe she would be out in the yard, or walking down the street. Even if she might not be there, I wanted to see the place.

Ann offered to drive me by the house over the weekend.

"No, I'd rather go some morning during the week," I said, adding, "—late morning, and I don't mind driving myself." I couldn't explain the urgency I felt about going to the place where my daughter lived. Wouldn't it make sense to make a careful, reasonable approach? No, a voice inside fairly shouted. I felt an overwhelming need to go there.

As soon as possible.

"It's really not a problem," she said. "I'll be glad to drive you."

"Can we go tomorrow?" I pressed.

The neighborhood was relatively close to the doctor's office where I had gone twenty-five years before. It would have been convenient for the adoptive mother to be his patient. I always wondered what kind of home my daughter lived in, and realized it did not matter as long as she was loved and got an education.

Ann drove slowly so I could take in the area and get a feeling about where she spent her childhood. We were only a few houses away from the house number I had, when I spotted the mailman walking along the sidewalk. "Ann!" I said. "Hurry, pull over. I want to talk to the mailman!"

I rolled down my window, and called over to him. "Excuse me, sir, but do the ...and I mentioned their last name...still live here? " He was a very pleasant, older gentleman, and came over to the car window so he could better hear me.

"They sure do," he said. "Lived here forever. Nice people. You looking for them?"

"No," I said, we're friends of their daughter, Charlene, and were just in the neighborhood."

"Well Charlene doesn't live there anymore. Got married year or so ago and moved away."

"Do you know where she moved to?" I asked, my heart sinking.

He had no idea, and no mail was being forwarded to her as far as he knew. "Just knock on the door and ask her parents where she lives," he said, "They'll be glad to give you her address." I would have loved to do just that. It would save me a lot of time. But somehow it just was not the proper thing to do. I thanked the mailman, sent from God, and we drove away.

Later that day I was at the county records office.

If she was married, they filed for a marriage license and those are public records. The marriage license application listed both of their names and both local addresses.

Mustering up almost brazen courage, I called her new husband's family home.

A man answered, and I told him I was a friend of Charlene's, but had misplaced her new address and phone number after she and Tom married. I had seen the name, Thomas, on the marriage license application.

He told me he was Tom's brother, and gave me her phone number and their address. She no longer lived here in Philadelphia. She was now in Annapolis, Maryland, by the Chesapeake Bay.

My heart skipped a beat, remembering the words of one psychic.

"You will find her closer to your home, and near water."

Fortified with that information, I sat down and

composed a new letter to her. I took into consideration the fact that she may not be aware she was adopted, and I accepted the fact that she may not want anything to do with me. I wanted to tell her so much more but it was not appropriate. I carefully re-read the letter, which stated simply: "I believe we are related, and if you are interested, you can contact me at…." and I gave her my name, address and phone number.

On a slushy, snowy Wednesday in February, I mailed the letter to her. The children's father was coming up that Friday to take them back to Virginia for the weekend, and for the first time, I would welcome their absence. Amid their pleas of, "Do we *have* to go again?" I said they did. "I have some important things to do." I wanted to be alone should she call.

I was slightly on edge much of Friday. I wondered if I had done the right thing. Had I interfered with her life by mailing that letter? The thought hounded me as I packed Jenny and Jon's overnight bags, then picked them up from school early so they would be back in Virginia before dark. Charles would be up around noon for them, and I was grateful he was coming up and I not have to drive to them to Virginia for the weekend this one time.

It was only noon, but I did not want to leave the house that day. I shoveled some of the slush off the patio out back and cleaned the bathrooms. I was afraid to run the vacuum because I might not hear the phone if it rang. I played with Kitty because she missed the children when they were gone. I was acting like a crazy person... or maybe, an *intuitive* one.

Who, in their right mind, would mail a letter on Wednesday and expect a response barely two days later, which is what I was doing. It did not make sense. Mail was not that fast, and even if she did get the letter on Friday, she might need some time to digest it. It could be weeks before I heard from her, if at all.

Walter dropped by to see if I needed anything, and I discouraged his staying for more than a few minutes. He knew I did not want him at my home when I was alone. I felt certain I was still being followed... by whom? or for whom? I could not risk his being there. Reluctantly, he complied with my wishes. He just wanted to make sure I was all right.

The winter sun had just gone down as I stood by the sliding glass doors leading to the patio but the sky was still beautiful as layers of color covered the horizon. The previous spring I had planted several evergreens around the patio and they were a stark contrast to the recent snow.

Such a peaceful sight in my anything but peaceful life. I just stood there wondering if my life would ever get back to normal.

The ringing of the phone jolted me out of my reverie.

My "Hello" was answered by a quiet voice. "Nancy?"

"Yes, this is she."

A moment of silence, then I heard the words my heart had ached to hear for many years, words that filled my eyes with tears and my soul with joy:

"You are my mother, aren't you?"

"Yes," I breathed. *"I am!"*

I could tell she was a bit emotional, but she was still more composed than I.

She wanted to meet as soon as possible, could we meet that Sunday? *In two days!*

"Of course we can," I told her, " Where would you like to meet?"

She suggested The Middleton Inn, in Annapolis, at 1 PM. I told her I wasn't sure where it was, but could probably find it.

I could hear the smile in her voice, "If you could find *me*, you can find the Middleton Inn."

She had a sense of humor! It made me forget the tears, and I smiled.

We decided to save our questions—*so many of them* — for Sunday.

Before hanging up, though, she hesitated. She wanted to tell me something.

"When I was trying to find you," she said, "I went to a psychic who told me, *Stop looking for your mother. She will find you.*"

To keep busy that Saturday, I drove up to Reading

to check on Sara in the nursing home. She was her usual complaining self, but it rolled off my head like water off a duck's back. On the way home I stopped at the Amish market in Morgantown to buy some flour for the weekly loaves of bread I was now baking. It seemed that the kneading and pounding of the dough against the butcher block table in the kitchen had a therapeutic effect on me, and besides, we all loved the taste of freshly baked bread.

Back at the townhouse, I tried on several outfits to wear on Sunday, hoping to find one that would help hide the pounds I had put on these past two years. I was never more than one hundred twenty, and I was sorry her first impression of me would be *fat*. And my hair was longer than I usually wore it… I was determined to get back to my real image as soon as possible.

Looking through my closet, I settled on a flattering mauve blazer and matching plaid skirt. I bought some flowers for her and decided against taking anything else. *After we meet, and if she is interested,* I thought, *I will show her my poetry, but certainly not for the first meeting.*

I called Walter to tell him I was leaving early the next morning and would pick up the children on my way back. In the meantime, would he please come over sometime Sunday and check on Kitty. I'd call him when I got home.

Saturday night I could hardly sleep.

CHAPTER 13

I WOKE UP earlier than usual that bright, sunny, but cold, Sunday morning in February. With ample time on my hands, I went to seven o'clock Mass at the Abbey... which would allow time for a quick breakfast back at my place before leaving for Annapolis.

My mind was flying in a million directions.

In the past year, I had become very attached to the Norbertine Abbey in Paoli. For me, it was a place of peace and comfort and I was fond of the Abbott, who was more than uplifting. But it was Father Dorff who had really opened my eyes. For several months I attended his classes on journaling, and found him to be a remarkable and wise man, always available for counseling or just listening. He once told us, "When you come to a crossroads in your life and are not sure which road to take, always *follow your heart*. It will never lead you astray."

One day, finding myself quite down, I called him to see if he had a few free moments. "I can see you right now," he said. I locked up the house and drove the short distance to the Abbey.

I was depressed and confused. I had been out of my home in Virginia for more than a year, and I missed it. Forced to rent a house in an area that I found unfriendly, I felt very alone. I was not sure where to go or what I should be doing.

I will never forget his words to me that morning. "Nancy, you are where you are *supposed* to be. You have a mission to accomplish, there is something you must do, and you can only do it if you are where you are. Whatever that mission is, you could not accomplish it if you were back in Virginia. That is why you are in Pennsylvania. Life always places us where we are supposed to be, at least for the moment."

That was not what I had hoped to hear, but on my way home I decided to dig my heels in and accept the fact I needed to be right where I was.

I realized how impossible it would have been for me to locate my daughter if I was living under Charles' roof back in Virginia. Father Dorff had been right. I did need to be right where I was at that time.

Even more astounding was the fact that I had *never*

even discussed my daughter or my search for her with Father Dorff. Since the Abbey had been such a comfort zone in my life I thought it only fitting to start this special day attending Mass there.

After a quick breakfast I left for Annapolis. Recently, I had often been late for a variety of reasons, but this *one day I absolutely could not be late*, so I allowed myself ample time for the two-and-a-half hour drive to Annapolis.

The roads were practically void of traffic that morning, and although there was considerable snow on the ground, the highways were clear.

Alone in the car, my mind took advantage of the solitude, allowing far too many thoughts and emotions to surface. Many of them drawing me back to a time and place I needed to forget.

For years, I had envisioned various scenarios for not only *our* first meeting but hopefully, for seeing her father again. I needed to push those thoughts aside, and concentrate fully on what I would say to my daughter who I would soon be meeting.

But the errant thoughts would not go away. They interjected themselves into my attempts to think and I began to feel overwhelmed. To quiet my racing mind, I turned the radio on. Always set to my favorite station, I did not have to search for soothing music.

Have you ever wondered why a certain song comes on the radio at the precise moment it does as though to validate the moment?

The music was relaxing and did quiet my thoughts, until I recognized the words of the song being sung… Lara's Theme, from Doctor Zhivago.

"…someday, we'll meet again, my love, someday, whenever the spring breaks through…."

I burst into tears. All the heartache and memories from twenty-five years ago surfaced with those words.

The movie, itself, had long-mirrored a part of my own life that stirred emotions with such sadness. I could not sit through the entire movie without crying.

I turned the radio off.

My face was a mess. Mascara was running down my cheeks and my eyes were red from crying. I could not let her see me like this. I was glad I had left early. I'd have time to re-do my face before our one o'clock meeting.

As I approached Annapolis, I found my way into the harbor without any problem. I had been at that very spot many times when I would go sailing with my wonderful friend, Father Murphy. We would pick up lunch at the Center City Market before sailing out on the bay, and I had never even noticed the Middleton Inn which was right across the street!

What I *did* remember, though, was that whenever I was near Annapolis, I would have strong thoughts of my daughter and the conversation would invariably lead to her. What I did not recognize back then was that—as my psychic friends explained - *I was picking up her energy.*

It was noon when I pulled into the parking lot across from the Inn.

Once inside, I went directly into the ladies room and refreshed my messy face before going back out into the open restaurant.

The place was relatively quiet with only a few couples sitting at the bar. I told the waiter I was waiting for someone, and would like a table near the door.

At about twelve-thirty, the place began to fill up and I found myself surrounded by happy, noisy couples who were now blocking my view of the door. I asked the waiter why there were so many people here in the middle of winter...this was a *boat* town.

"Ma'am," he said, "It's Valentine's Day, and everyone comes out to celebrate."

How could I have forgotten!—and I did not have a Valentine for her. I felt awful!

Our first meeting, and on Valentine's Day! and no card! And it was too late to buy one. At least I had some flowers. What will she think?

Unable to see the door because of the crowd, I was now afraid I would miss her. So I moved further into the room, where I had a better view.

One-fifteen came and still no sight of her. Maybe she was here somewhere in the crowd and since she had no idea what I looked like, might have thought I left.

I was beginning to get anxious.

Every time the door opened, I craned my neck, looking for the face I had seen in the yearbook two weeks before.

About one-thirty I saw the door open and a young woman walk in, alone. The first thing I noticed was her full head of dark, curly hair. She was scanning the room as though looking for someone she could not possibly recognize. And then, she looked right at me, and above the noise of the crowd, I could hear the lilt in her voice, and my name....

"Nancy?"

I weaved through the crowd toward her. There was no denying she was the face in the yearbook, but no photo could capture that smile...the smile of a man I once loved.

Instinctively, we hugged each other and I felt a deep, warm connection to this slip of a girl, who—here in my arms now, no longer a dream image but a real live girl—seemed so fragile. I was afraid she would break if I hugged her too tightly.

But I did not want to let go of her.

No matter how hard I tried to control my mind, I could not prevent the tears that mingled with hers as we wrapped our arms around each other. We tried to talk but were drowned out by the noisy crowd.

"I know a quiet place down the road where we *can* talk," she said. "Ok if we go there?" I agreed, and we navigated through the crowd toward the door. "First, let me grab my coat from the rack," I said.

As I approached the front of the room, I was suddenly aware of the music, which I had not noticed before, and it appeared someone had turned up the volume... I stopped dead in my tracts. *Impossible.*

The mournful theme song from *Doctor Zhivago* was playing once again, its words tweaking my heartstrings.

"...You'll come to me, out of the long ago, warm as the wind, soft as the kiss of snow...."

This was too much. I lifted my coat off the rack, wiped the tears away, then slipped the coat over my mauve jacket. She was waiting for me by the door, and probably thinking to herself, *"She sure is a teary one."*

As for me, the thought briefly flitted through my mind: *Beyond this realm, and using music, were unseen entities letting me know that their mission was accomplished?*

Now my tears were tears of joy, not longing.

I took her hand and we walked out the door.

Once out in the daylight, I saw she was wearing a mauve skirt with a matching jacket.

"I am so sorry I was late," she said. "I always *try* to be on time, but somehow I just wind up being late."

I smiled and thought, you *come by that honestly.*

And then she told me that the reason she was late is that just as she was going out the door, her adoptive mother called. Obviously, she could not tell her why she was in a hurry, so she chatted briefly, even though this would make her late.

A coincidence?

I followed her down the highway to the restaurant she had suggested. It was rather empty that afternoon allowing us plenty of privacy. We ordered something to drink but neither of us ever touched it.

As I handed her the flowers I brought for her, I apologized for not having a Valentine because I had completely forgotten it was Valentines Day.

"Is today Valentines Day?" she said. "I forgot it, too." She then added, "I got engaged on Valentine's Day."

I countered: "And I found out I was pregnant with you on Valentine's Day."

From then on, it would become our anniversary.

We talked intermittently ...trying to cram two lifetimes into two hours. I tried to answer her many questions with total honesty. Then, when she asked me how I found her, I told her.

After a few moments she said something I did not expect to hear, "We could have made it, you know, if you had kept me."

"And if I had died, as they'd told me I might?" I replied. "I could not risk your being uncared for."

But beyond the reasoned response, I recognized the pain she must have felt by being given up for adoption. It couldn't come anywhere near the pain I had experienced over the years. *Or so I wrongfully believed!*

Yes, we might have made it, but we are not meant to foresee some things.

A little later she asked me, "What would you like me to call you?"

I wanted to say, "Mom," but out of deference to her adoptive mother I replied, "Nancy is fine."

Toward the end of our meeting, she asked me what I wanted from her.

"I want only to know you, have *you* know me. I want you to know you were born out of love, and were *not, out of convenience,* given away. I want you to know there's a place in my life for you and I hope there is one—even a small one—in your life for me."

I also gave her a very brief overview of my life at the moment and answered a few more questions.

And then, to be fair, I let her know I would accept her decision regarding any future meetings. I'd learned from others that these first meetings, with so little preparation, can oftentimes be traumatic. If she did not wish to pursue a relationship, as painful as it would be for me, I would abide by her decision.

At least, I had found her...was able to see her and touch her...and if that was all I would ever have, I would have to accept it.

There was so much more we wanted to know about each other, but we both had commitments... and it was time to go. So afraid I would not see her again, I was reluctant to leave, and I sensed she shared a similar reluctance.

This was apparent once we were outside, standing on the windy hillside. Neither of us wanted to be the first to walk away. We were having a difficult time saying goodbye.

Still, anxious thoughts began swirling around in my head. *What if she does not want to see me again and is just delaying so she can get one last look at me.*

Even so, I hugged her goodbye once more and reassured her that she could take her time deciding if she wanted to meet again. Whatever it was, I would abide by her decision. For *I* had been the one to invade *her* life.

"Thank you, Nancy, I do need to think about it," she said. I had a feeling her doubts had more to do with her adoptive parents than with me. After all, she *had* sought the help of a psychic once when *she was looking for me.*

In my work with adult adoptees, I found that many were fearful of hurting their adoptive parents if they searched for the birth parents. While I understood this, I still believed she and I could bridge that fear.

It was too early to tell if I would ever see her again, but there *was* one clue.

As we stood there on the blustery hillside, waiting to go our separate ways, she reached over and tucked a stray, windblown lock of my hair back into place.

She smiled, turned, and was gone. She probably could not see me, but I waved goodbye and watched her get into her car.

Please, God, don't let this be the last time I see her. There is so much more she needs to know.

As I got into my own car, I realized that without saying a word, she had just put my worst fear to rest. I simply felt it in that last loving gesture.

Within the next few days, I wrote a long narrative poem, detailing my thoughts and feelings on "Our First Meeting." In it I wrote:

I am whole once again,
a part of me found,
the part I had left in the past.

I decided to mail it to her. Should she not want to see me again at least she would know how I felt.

The day I mailed my poem to her I received... a letter from her. With her permission, I quote this verse.

I love you more than I ever knew, I need you in my world,
Of all the times I thought of you, I never knew you cared.
I hoped, I dreamed that someday soon, I'd see you at my door,
I'd welcome you with open arms, as if we'd met before.

One day, a few years later, she asked me if I minded if she called me "Mom." "It just feels more natural," she said.

EPILOGUE

SOON AFTER MY DAUGHTER, Charlene, and I met, she visited us in Paoli, where she met her two younger half-siblings. I then made a few trips to Annapolis to visit her, and she met the older children a bit later. Slowly, she and I began to bridge the gap created by her adoption.

We allowed time to heal our wounds and gradually came to know each other, often reveling in our many similarities.

I smiled when I found out she played the violin… having heard it so often in utero, she connected to the familiar sound naturally. When I was pregnant with her, I often listened to my favorite Montavani records. The beautiful string orchestra was soothing and I would sometimes hum along with the music. So, it was not surprising that she would be drawn to it.

Some of the revelations were stunning.

One day, while she and I were comparing notes, she said to me, out of the blue, "There was a time during my marriage when I desperately needed you. I was reaching out to you, hoping you could hear me. I kept calling for you. I would cry out, 'Mother, Mother,' over and over again."

We later determined it was the same time frame back in Virginia several years before, when I was hearing someone call for "Mother, Mother."

Another revelation reinforced a gut feeling I had had at the time….After my daughter told her adoptive parents that we had met, her mother mentioned that she was not surprised because the doctor who delivered her, the same one that told me he "did not keep adoption records," had contacted the adoptive mother to let her know I was *inquiring about the child.*

The summer after we met, my long time friend, Father Murphy arranged for my daughter and me to spend a few days at the beach house of friends of his in New Jersey.

He thought it would give us private time to get to know each other. While there she said to me one day, "My parents and I would always go to the Jersey shore every summer."

"Where did you go?" I asked her, holding my breath. It was the town next to Avalon where the children and I spent a month every summer.

When I had visited the psychic in Philadelphia—the one who told me I would "find my daughter, but closer to my home and near water"—I noticed several framed letters on her wall. One was from Frank Sinatra, a few from other well- known figures, all thanking her for her help.

This re-enforced my confidence in her, and enabled me to more readily accept some of her revelations. For starters, the first thing this very business-like woman had said to me was, "There are three men around you right now creating havoc in your life. Let's see what this is all about." I might mention that up to this point, all I had told her was my first and last name. Nothing more.

"These men have been with you in other lifetimes." she said. "One is your present husband. You have been connected to him in other lives and in each one, you tried to get away from him. Once, he bought you as a slave, and when you ran away he either shot you or *had* you shot. You came together in this life so that you could free yourself from him *properly*. That is why you had to marry him so you could legally free yourself from him. You cannot continue to run away from him."

I could barely keep quiet but did not want to interrupt her.

For years, I had a recurring dream of being chased and being shot... sometimes running through fields, hiding in a building, or under a piece of furniture... never actually *feeling* being shot... just knowing I was... and then waking up frightened, but relieved it was only a dream.

And…Charles would often call me "slave." "Slave," do this, or "slave" get me that. I would recoil and tell him that not even in *jest*, to call me that, because I truly did feel like his slave. But more scary is the comment he would make when I refused to move back home. "Why? Are you afraid I'm going to shoot you?"

If, indeed, we do live more than one life on earth, I wondered, *is it possible that something will trigger a memory from another life?*

The psychic continued. "The other man is foreign, German, I believe. Is there a German man in your life now? You weren't supposed to meet him in this life, however, circumstances brought you two together. He always tried to protect you in those lives, but you kept pushing him away.

"I do see the two of you during the Viking period… he was always a warrior," she interjected. "In that life, he stole you from your husband and took you for his wife. That husband is your *present* husband. These two men have been together in many lifetimes and have brought their hatred for each other with them into this life. They need to resolve it or it will continue to plague their souls."

Again, I was taken aback by her words.

After the children and I moved into Walter's house, Charles repeatedly made the absurd and ridiculous comment to Walter, "You stole my wife."

And on top of that, Walter was convinced that I was

once his Viking Queen. He told me that when he saw me for the first time years before, he'd been visibly shaken, because he felt he recognized me.

I was walking up the wide steps of another hospital that day in 1955, when I noticed a man leaning against the wall, smoking a cigarette. As I got closer I realized he had been staring at me. He stamped his cigarette out, and came toward me. We were face to face...and he was shaking. He had a heavy accent, but I could understand him.

"I am sorry, I thought you were someone else," he said, not taking his eyes off me.

I'd felt a strange feeling in my gut... almost as if I wanted to flee. I was not afraid of him, but recognized something I could not put my finger on. It was eerie.

He then walked down the steps, turning once to glance back at me. I watched him get into his car. He turned around and looked up at me once again before driving off.

This was a complete stranger, so why did something inside me click the way it did and why was I standing there waiting to make sure he left?

Later that evening, when Steve, Charlene's father, came by to see me, he brought along a friend he wanted me to meet.

And then he then introduced me to his friend, Walter... the man on the steps.

Sitting in Valerie's office, where I had gone for enlightenment, I was beginning to think I was in a movie theatre. Such stories. Where were they coming from? How could she know these things? But scarier was the fact, it all made sense. In fact, her readings clarified many unexplainable issues.

This woman did not fool around. She spoke as though she was simply relaying to me what she was being shown.

"The third man...he's not active in your life right now," she said," but he is very much involved." That was Steve.

"This was a true love relationship," she said. "You were husband and wife in several other life times, and you recognized each other immediately when you met in this life. But it was not to be. There was another reason you met."

I asked her if we would ever meet again.

"Yes, I do see you meeting, "she answered. "But, you will look into his eyes and know," *Not again in this lifetime.*

That statement concerned me. Up until then, she had my attention, but now I was beginning to doubt everything she had previously said to me... because I was confident that if I ever saw Steve again I could never feel that way.

Some years later, Steve and I finally did meet. After my daughter located him, he began to call me regularly. His wife had "left him and gone back to Germany," he told me. The phone calls between us had sounded fine, and I loved hearing his voice. One day he asked if I would fly up to meet him because he could not get away. "It would mean so much if you would come up," he had said.

For years I had dreamt of that moment! I could not wait for the plane to land. But when he met me at the airport, I was shocked as soon as I saw him.

It was not fear, or disappointment, but the realization that the psychic was right.

His eyes were the first thing I noticed. In place of the warm, smiling, loving eyes that had captured my being long ago, I was looking into the bulging eyes of someone who was obviously *very* emotionally ill.

"You will look into his eyes and know, 'Not again, not in this lifetime.'"

Despite the disappointment I felt over his condition, the three of us eventually did meet later, but briefly. Steve came to Virginia twice for a visit. A year later, he died a very sad death. When my daughter, Steve and I met in Philadelphia on one of those visits, he took me to meet his mother, Molly, who I immediately found delightful. She was a lovely woman and we spoke frequently on the phone after that visit. After Steve died, she begged me to take her to where her son was buried, and I promised her I would.

But Molly died before I could fulfill that promise.

Shortly after she died, I had a reading from a medium who asked if I knew anyone named Molly. When I affirmed that I did, she gave me this message: "Molly wants you to know, *they are both fine.* That's what she keeps saying." *Tell her we are both fine."*

I felt so relieved, and so happy that she got in touch with me. I can't wait to meet her in the next life, we had such a brief time together here. She's the Jewish mother-in-law I never had.

But I had something more to learn about Psychic readings. When two souls are closely connected, it is possible for the reader to inadvertently pick up information from one and apply it to the other. This phenomenon occurred shortly before I left Philadelphia.

One day I called the woman who had read for me in Philadelphia to ask her a question...but she interrupted me. "Stop," she said. "You must go back to Virginia soon...as soon as you can. Otherwise things will become very difficult for you financially. Your husband is going to die suddenly. I see him having a heart attack and dying in the emergency room. It looks like within a month. It is not too far away," she said in a very grim voice.

It was the end of summer, my lease was up in three weeks and I had planned to renew it. She had been so accurate in the past, I felt I needed to heed her warning, so notified the Realtor I would not be renewing.

The children were devastated but I promised them that we would move back as soon as we could. That comforted Jenny for a while, but Jon insisted on going to Valley Forge Military Academy. "If you make me go back I will run away," he said. I had sufficient funds to pay his tuition so I allowed him to stay and enroll at Valley Forge. Returning to Virginia was a terrible decision for all of us, but I thought it was the only way, given the prediction. I would definitely need to get a handle on the finances ahead of time and returning seemed to be the only way.

So, with a very heavy heart, I began to pack. I decided to store all of my furniture and belongings for the time being and only take essential papers and clothes with us. Walter was hysterical. "Have you lost your mind?" he shouted. He was obviously devastated. I also knew that I could never negotiate a divorce with Walter in the picture, but now this news! In any event, I would need to be back in Virginia, at least temporarily.

Charles was delighted. *He began to tell everyone that I begged him to let me come home.*

And I could not tell *anyone* the reason I was doing this.

The week before the move, with the house already rented to new tenants and the movers scheduled, Charles showed up, unannounced. Surprised, I foolishly thought he had come to help, but no...he was "distraught." I asked him what was wrong.

"I just buried my best friend this morning," he said. Paul(not his name) had called Charles a couple nights before, with chest pain. Charles told him to call 911 and said he would meet him at the hospital. But he was too late, Paul had already died in the ER... Just as Valerie had seen... but she had picked up, not my *husband's* energy, but that of his inseparable friend.

I was devastated...but another intuition of mine had just been confirmed.

My own devastation was about to undo me. But it was not over. When Walter, who was reluctantly helping me pack, attempted to move my filing cabinet, a drawer slid out and he saw a document I had intentionally kept from him.

Shortly after I moved into Walter's house, my jealous husband had contacted a government agency attempting to have Walter deported. The document confirmed this. When Walter saw the document, he called the agency, made an appointment and insisted I accompany him downtown to their headquarters. It was not a very pleasant meeting. After much discussion and threats from Walter, the Agency admitted they had not only been following me for three years, but had also tapped my phone.

Their reason? Based on my husband's description of Walter, I might be 'passing secret documents to the enemy.' They apologized for the intrusion and later added, "We ceased all surveillance when the agents reported back that all you did was visit a sick relative, take the children to school and shop. We realized this was nothing more than the antics of a jealous husband." A *sick*, jealous husband, I might add.

I had been right, all along. I *sensed* I was being followed all those years, it was not my imagination. But I was outraged that my phone had been tapped.

By returning to my home in Virginia, I had lost my grounds for divorce, and once again, found myself trapped. My outrage over the surveillance was overshadowed by the depression that followed but I managed to recover and eventually divorced Charles.

After thirty years out of the work force, I accepted a position in a Physicians office, where I am still employed and I began to forge a new life. I see my six children as often as I can, and I am happy.

I visit Anne Gehman at sporadic intervals, and always find welcome, reassuring messages when I do. Recently, during one of her group readings, she asked if anyone knew a man named "Walter" on the other side. No one else did.

"He was an electrician, but not the kind that works around a house, but someone who might climb high tension power lines," she said. "Does anyone know someone like this?" I said, "He might be a friend of mine."

Walter worked on the extremely high-tension power lines along the Schuylkill Expressway in Philadelphia when I knew him. Anne smiled and said, "Yes, it is *you* he is addressing."

"He wants you to know you have an electrical problem in your house. It is serious and if he were here, he would fix it for you."

Shortly after the reading, I had an electrician check the house where he found the problem and repaired it.

In a private session recently, Anne said to me, "Your husband is having a difficult time progressing in the next life. He is filled with remorse over this past life and it is holding him back. He needs your forgiveness so he can move ahead. Please do this for him."

I told her I had already forgiven him, but I would do so again. He no longer had a hold on me, and I wanted him to be free to move on with his new life on the other side.

It is an honorable thing to pray for the dead. They need the energy from our prayers to assist them as they move ahead in their new life. For no one is *really* dead, since we continue to grow in the next life.

And I believe that when we come back, we do so in order to allow the soul to grow. Here, we meet those we have known before, either to help one another, or make amends for something, or to learn.

I may have had to learn a painful lesson by giving up a child I wanted, or to find my own strength, or to learn patience, or maybe all of the above. She may have needed to learn something by being adopted. In any event it appears that we are all connected in one way or another to everyone we meet in this life.

Another example of connectedness. I found out one day that all three of my daughters have had the same recurring dream that I had over a period of years. Strange, but once we mentioned the dream to one another, it never recurred.

I am at the edge of the sea, and looking out into the distance, I see a huge wall of water coming at me. It is a tsunami. My children are with me, and I am holding them close to me, praying that we will be saved. I am trying to protect them from drowning.

I always woke up soaking wet from perspiration, then felt relieved it was only a dream. Or was it Atlantis? Or Lemuria?

However you think of the Other Side, our Spirit Guides, or the Spirit World, some things will always remain difficult to explain. I only relay to the reader my own experiences and how I grew to find comfort, healing and help from this unseen world.

We *may* only live once, but it seems irrational to believe that Our Creator gives us but one chance for salvation. We do good, we go to Heaven. We do bad things, we go to Hell. I am not alone in believing differently. I believe that even in the afterlife there is opportunity for the soul to grow, for I also believe, as I have been taught, that there are many levels in Heaven. And hopefully, after this present sojourn, we will find ourselves on a higher level when we go back home.

For now, I wish to honor those unseen, but elevated

souls who have come to my aid and assistance in this lifetime.

For all your help and continued guidance, I *Thank you*, with deepest gratitude and humility.

Nancy Hannan

ACKNOWLEGEMENTS

ONCE AGAIN, I thank my writing coach and editor, David Hazard for his unwavering faith in, and dedication to my writing this book. We always seemed to be on the same page, but if I began to slide off, he gently pulled me back.

I am also deeply grateful to Peter Gloege, our book designer, without whom these pages might never be seen. You both have inspired me to continue writing.

I must also acknowledge my long ago friends from the Adoption Forum of Philadelphia back in the Eighties who guided, reassured, and encouraged me in my search.

And most importantly, my children, who stood beside me those difficult years. It was their support and encouragement that enabled me to search for their sister, even as I disrupted their lives. I will be forever grateful for the comfort and reassurance they gave me.